EXETER

The Golden Years

Peter Thomas

HALSGROVE

First published in Great Britain in 2003

Dedicated to my loving mother Ivy

British Library Cataloguing-in-Publication Data
A CIP record for this title is available from the British Library

ISBN 1 84114 294 8

HALSGROVE
Halsgrove House
Lower Moor Way
Tiverton, Devon EX16 6SS
Tel: 01884 243242
Fax: 01884 243325
email: sales@halsgrove.com
website: www.halsgrove.com

Printed and bound in Great Britain by Bookcraft Ltd, Midsomer Norton

Contents

Acknowledgements

I would like to acknowledge the following people for their help with this book: Mr J Borne, Mrs R Cartwright, Mrs A Collins, Drew Pearce of Exeter, Mr E Hopkins, Mrs S Wilcox, the Westcountry Studies Library (Devon County Council); to Mrs Lorna Till for constant help and support; the people of Exeter who have supported the ISCA Historical Photographic Collection.

The Isca Collection

The Isca Collection was first started in 1974 by the author after discovering that a huge collection of photographic plates and negatives was liable to be disposed of. The resource was the work of Henry Wykes and his assistant Marjorie Hockmuth. Following the closure of the Wykes Studio in Northernhay Place, Exeter, in 1974, the author obtained the complete collection of some 42 000 half-plate negatives. Examination of the records revealed that they showed Exeter as it had been from around 1910 up to 1970. It was obvious that the work was of vital importance to the history of Exeter and started the author's passion for collecting photographic records of the City of Exeter. To date the Isca Collection includes negatives, prints, slides, albums, books and other items of interest.

In the following years numerous exhibitions have been undertaken, assistance given to TV documentary makers, along with radio interviews and press coverage. The collection has been responsible for a number of publications to date including *Old Exeter, Aspects of Exeter* (co-author Jacqueline Warren), *The House That Moved, Exeter in Old Postcards,* and *Exeter in Old Photographs*. It has also assisted with illustrations for a variety of publications. The collection is the largest private archive of Exeter records and is registered with The Royal Photographic Society in the British Photographic Record, a directory of historical photographic collections.

Exeter - The Golden Years

1940 to 1960 & Beyond

The bombing of Exeter in May 1942 was a major turning point that changed the face of the city, both in the immediate aftermath and in the rebuilding that followed. The renewal of the city's heart was to take nearly thirty years to complete, during which time Exonians became familiar with bombed sites, removal of buildings and a fundamental change to the city in which they had grown up. This situation occurred all over the country as populations struggled to come back to normality. It instigated a time for radical change as older aspects of towns and cities were swept away in the name of progress. For many these were exciting times, ushering in a possible new era of modern living and, hopefully, prosperity. The period from the 1940s to the 1960s is often referred to as The Golden Years but, in the case of Exeter, redevelopment continued well into the late 1970s.

On 4 May 1942 approximately one-third of Exeter's centre was destroyed, including High Street, Bedford Street, Catherine Street, Bampfylde Street, Paris Street, Sidwell Street, Newtown, Fore Street and South Street. It was one of 17 recorded raids on Exeter, with the former being the most destructive. A large contingent of military help was brought in to clear the streets, assist in subduing fires, pulling down unstable buildings and generally helping the public. In the weeks and months that followed, the whole of the central area was cleared, which involved pulling down the remains of the standing west side of the famous Georgian Bedford Circus, the removal of St Lawrence Church in High Street and the demolition of the frontage of the Commercial Union building, a noted landmark. One the most tragic removals was that of Dellers Café in Bedford Street, Exeter's most famous eating and social establishment. Its unique architectural shell still stood and could have been saved. For a considerable period of time it was possible to stand at the corner of the London Inn Square (today Boots) and to look to the Cathedral with no buildings blocking the view. No such scene had been witnessed before in the whole of the city's history and this scene was to be the most famous propaganda image relating to Exeter in the Second World War. Many of the city's prime historical buildings had been lost and now a new era of irrevocable change was dawning.

Determined to make rapid progress after the blitz of May 1942, the City Council commissioned the services of the Town Planner, Thomas Sharp, who was appointed in October 1943 and quickly set about drawing up plans to recreate the city. By December 1945 his plan for Exeter had been prepared and was exhibited in the shell of the City Library. The exhibition was opened on 28 December by the Minister of Town & Country Planning, Mr L Silkin, and ran for two weeks, its focus being 'The Growth of Exeter the Region', 'Traffic', 'Beauty', 'The Blight of the Blitz' and 'Employment'. The outline plan included building up the central area, industrial proposals and a central road. The exhibition was visited by 28 035 people between 29 December and 19 January. Thomas Sharp, who was president of the Town Planning Institute proposed that 'Outside the City Wall should be a green moat of open space.' By early 1946 the compulsory purchase of blitzed areas was agreed and the redevelopment plan approved.

In March of the same year a new initiative was discussed to assist in helping businesses to continue trading. This involved the possible erection of temporary shops in the central area, deemed as an urgent requirement, but traders said permanent premises were preferable. Agreement was reached in June but it was suggested that the shortage of labour would delay the works. In September 1946 it was announced that 54 shops would be built. At the top of Southernhay, joining Eastgate, 32 shops would be erected, with 22 more on the site of the Lower Market. The scheme would cost

£33 000 and delivery of materials was expected in nine weeks.

In December 1946 it was stated that in order to complete Thomas Sharp's plan in its entirety, properties still standing in the central area would have to be acquired. However, Thomas Sharp's vision was to run into difficulties in relation to the changes suggested for Eastgate Square. The proposal was for a large rectangular gyratory system revolving around a landscaped focal point. This was opposed, and in June 1948 a new concept was put forward by the City Architect, H B Rowe. In July 1949 the City Council accepted the new Eastgate Scheme and it was highly praised.

In the same period decisions were being taken relating to the development of the Marsh Barton Trading Estate. This would result in the use of farm land at Alphington being used for industrial units and would be adjacent to the Livestock Market that had been relocated from Bonhay Road in 1939.

In September 1948 the Government gave the go-ahead for rebuilding to begin in 1949 and the Council quickly unanimously passed a plan outlining a three-year programme of rebuilding in the blitzed central areas, at a cost of £1 100 000. It would include works in High Street and Southernhay, with some token rebuilding on Sidwell Street. Schedules would start with 1949/50 High Street; 1950/51 High Street & Sidwell Street; 1951/52 High Street, Sidwell Street, Fore Street and South Street.

A small ceremony took place on 7 January 1949, with the Mayor, Alderman W T Slader, hammering in the first peg, to realign Bedford Street.

An integral aspect of Thomas Sharp's plan was a freeway to the north of the city, but this was deemed to involve excessive costs and was opposed. An alternative road to the south was put forward by City Architect Harold Rowe, and City Engineer John Brierley, the route accepted by the City Council. It would be responsible for the removal of much of the south side of the city.

By now there had been much discussion and many delays over the new proposals, but to get the rebuilding under way it was necessary to apply for an allocation of steel, as this was strictly regulated. An allocation of 450 tons was ordered, which might, the City Council suggested, arrive in January 1950, but no fixed date for rebuilding could be given.

Architects' drawings for the new city centre were now being produced, with modern designs for Colsons' department store (at St Stephen's) and the Pearl Assurance, High Street.

In the latter part of the year an idea was recommended for a pedestrian shopping precinct. It would consist of a 'colonnade', under which shoppers could be protected, a completely new concept for Exeter. It was also suggested that work could start on the north-west side in 1951/52, and a drawing appeared in local newspapers in December 1949.

During this year it was decided that a special commemorative feature should be built to mark the start of rebuilding the city. It was to be constructed on the site of the proposed shopping precinct and exactly aligned to the North Tower of Exeter Cathedral. Thomas Sharp had recommended that the precinct should be laid out to give a fine view of Exeter Cathedral, with no obstruction. On 21 October 1949 HRH Princess Elizabeth visited the city and named the future new shopping precinct 'Princesshay'. She stood on a purpose-built feature that still retains a plaque commemorating the start of rebuilding.

At the end of 1949 it was reported that the first building stones might be laid in the New Year, but labour was still limited, together with some materials. The work of constructing deep sewers had been completed before the eighth anniversary of the blitz. New housing was also designated for Countess Wear and Stoke Hill.

In January 1950 more temporary shops were suggested, for erection at Cheeke Street and Summerland Street. Each would be 22 x 70ft and self-erected. Every shop would have a seven-year lease that would expire on 30 June 1957, at a cost of £80 per annum.

In High Street the first contract was realised with a £100 000 project for five shops and offices. It was to be called Pearl Assurance House.

New plans for Sidwell Street were also released, based on a 4ft-wide central island running up the street. It was not well received. After much criticism of the project the City Council returned the plans to the planning committee, citing fears of rising costs and the possibility of creating a bottleneck.

In March 1950 the well-known store, Colsons, in High Street was in the news. The company, established in 1792, had substantial premises almost adjacent to St Stephen's Church in High Street. Two floors had been destroyed during the night of 4 May and it was now suggested that it was more economical to rebuild, with up to £150 000 being paid by the War Damages Commission. Another well-known company, Marks & Spencer, had their Fore Street property totally destroyed but were to rebuild on a prestigious High Street location at the corner of Castle Street (today Russell & Bromley shoes). The store, measuring 110 x 112ft, was scheduled to open on 4 May, the eighth anniversary of the blitz and its construction was eagerly watched by interested shoppers. At this time the new Commercial Union building, also in High Street, was nearing completion.

In June 1950 an extra £4 million was granted by the Government to assist with the rebuilding of blitzed cities, of which Exeter was to receive £350 000.

The foundation stone of the first building in High Street was laid by Exeter MP John Maude in July 1950, and the Pearl Assurance House started. New premises were proposed for the Devon & Exeter Saving Bank in Bedford Street.

The demolition and clearance of city-centre buildings created another problem, this being how to dispose of the rubble. Bricks had been used to infill cellars and basements in order to construct new roads, but two sites were to be earmarked for the general dumping of substantial amounts of brick and waste. One was the small valley that led from Barnfield Road to Magdalen Bridge. An orchard that occupied the valley, with a small cottage called Fairfield Park, was a favourite place to scrump apples for local children. But the whole valley was to be lost as it was filled up with rubble and became the base for the new Inner Bypass. Further rubble was deposited at Belle Isle Sewage Works, adjacent to Trews Weir Bridge. Massive granite blocks from the Lower Market were also taken out of the city and dumped into local rivers to assist with preventing erosion of the banks.

At the end of January 1951 the Clock Tower in Queen Street became the centre of hot debate when a new road-improvement scheme that would have mean its demolition was put forward. A campaign was organised to save it and ideas of re-erecting it elsewhere suggested, the cost of which was estimated at £11–12 000. The demolition was shelved.

In late March the newspapers announced that the first new shops would be opening in the High Street. These would include costumiers Harolds, hosiers Sebley and Woodleys' shoe shop. In April drawings of the proposed new buildings for the top of Princesshay were published and in June work started on the eastern block. It would consist of 12 shops, of which six faced the High Street.

Plans were now to be discussed for a new service road at the rear of the Telephone Exchange, involving the widening of New Buildings and the appropriation of land from Rougemont Gardens. The project would also necessitate the removal of an historic building from Gandy Street that had been used as auction rooms. In July 1951 new plans relating to the development of Exeter up until 1971 were released, with estimated costs of £7 500 000, and Exeter Chamber of Commerce put forward an idea for two new bridges over the River Exe.

In August Lloyds Bank in High Street was under construction and proved to be the longest building project to complete owing to the construction of special storage rooms with 2ft-thick walls. In early November traffic schemes for the next thirty years were considered, to include Exe Bridge, Paris Street, Cowick Street and Alphington Street. In late December the cutting of a deep new service road for Princesshay was instigated and designed to run from Bedford Street eastwards at the rear of the new precinct buildings.

In late February 1952 trees were being thinned opposite the Royal Devon and Exeter Hospital to allow for the construction of a car park on the site of the old Trinity Green graveyard. A shelter and toilets were also to be built.

Exeter's emerging new persona now came under fire and in August 1952 the *Architects' Journal* deplored the city's efforts as 'an architectural compromise, neither absolutely modern nor fake antique. The design lacks conviction', whilst offering congratulations on the speed. Further comment stated: 'The need is for architects to clarify their minds as to what is good modern architecture and then set about educating the public and therefore the client, to appreciate it.' More comment hit the press in November, with the statement: 'Exeter is very disappointing.'

In late December a report by the eminent archaeologist Lady Aileen Fox was published, suggesting that excavations pointed to Exeter having been founded in AD50–54. The destruction of Exeter had laid bare large tracts of land in the central area, enabling easier access to archaeological remains. Lady Fox had become a familiar figure in the city centre, undertaking digs with voluntary helpers. Her pioneering work was to lay the foundations for the uncovering and recording of Exeter's early history on an unprecedented scale.

In mid-January 1953 a High Street property was threatened with demolition. The shoe shop Barratts, adjacent to Colsons, a double-gabled seventeenth-century building, was declared unsafe. The proposal was to reconstruct the sites of Barratts and Colsons in a Tudor-style building. This did not transpire and Barratts was demolished and rebuilt in a modern style. The corner site of High Street and Bedford Street was under construction at this time and was to replace the demolished shell of Dellers Café and Lloyds Bank.

On the opposite corner with Catherine Street the new Martins Bank was under construction. In April 1954 Fore Street and South Street were a focus of attention with preparation taking place for the building of South Street, and by August the west side of the latter was also under way.

In mid-June 1954 it was announced that furnishing company Mark Rowe's newly built store would open the next day 22 June 1954. The company's previous building had stood in High Street on the same site and displayed a famous statue of Henry VII on its frontage. All was destroyed in the blitz on 4 May 1942.

In March 1955 No. 16 Edmund Street hit the news with a headline 'To go or not to go'. The early-fifteenth-century timber-framed building stood in the way of the Western Way Inner Bypass. Against this threat of demolition, the Ministry of Housing and Local Government placed a provisional order on the building to restrict its removal, alteration or extension. Around the same time Roman archaeological remains were uncovered in South Street. In Bedford Street the new Barclays Bank, the Exeter Savings Bank and Princesshay were completed in August, with a garden feature being laid out on the west side.

Posing a persistent problem were the two bottlenecks of Eastgate Square and Exe Bridge but a new proposal for Eastgate was turned down. By early December life was returning to the High Street with two-way traffic using the thoroughfare.

In October 1956 the state of play of other historic buildings was noted. Nos 11 and 12 Cathedral Close had almost been totally destroyed on 25 April 1942, with only the ancient arched stone doorway left standing. As some of the most important buildings in the Cathedral Close a reconstruction project had been initiated and at this point was approximately halfway to completion.

On 14 October of the following year it was reported that a Blue Boy statue had been placed in Princesshay, to commemorate St John's School which had closed in 1931. Two of these statues had stood at the High Street gateway to the former school. The new pedestrian precinct was constructed where the playground had been.

At the end of October the City Engineer put forward a scheme for a new bridge over the River Exe at a cost of £605 000, this being accepted by the Council in mid-November. In the central area the new Post Office building in Bedford Street was well under way. In Sidwell Street the north side was almost complete.

Paris Street roundabout was to come into its own in early February 1957 with roadworks nearly complete. Buses were still using the old tram depot in Heavitree Road next to the swimming baths.

In mid-January 1958 some the city's prime historic buildings were thrown into the spotlight when they were threatened with removal. A proposed road-widening scheme for High Street put Nos 226 and 227 in danger, creating an angry reaction from the public and noted bodies. A printed article decried the citizens of Exeter 'as a city of fools' if they allowed such destruction to take place. In February the *Western Times* vacated 226 High Street, taking up residence in 160 Sidwell Street, as the building had been acquired for road-widening purposes. The threat to the two buildings provoked a reaction from respected historian Professor W G Hoskins. In June Professor Hoskins spoke out against the demolition of the two High Street buildings, stating categorically 'The buildings are genuine and not fakes', as had been suggested from some quarters.

The bombing of the Lower Market and Corn Exchange had removed an important aspect from the top of Fore Street but the impressive Italian-style granite exterior survived the blitz. A plan put forward in 1958 suggested creating a new building at a cost of £220 000.

By the end of October 1958 three-quarters of the city centre had been rebuilt and a further scheme was put forward to create a prestigious Civic Centre. It would involve the demolition of the Civic Hall in Queen Street, the Higher Market, Waterbeer Street and North Street. Once again, however, the project did not transpire.

In mid-December it was agreed that the city would build its own bus station at Paris Street and in March 1959 it was agreed that a simplified Eastgate junction would be built, starting in 1960 and taking approximately twelve to eighteen months to complete. In the early part of the year South Street was cleared of old buildings at the junction with Palace Gate to allow widening and improvements to its appearance. Five shop units and four maisonettes were to replace the north side, and on the south side, six shop units and three two-bedroom maisonettes were to be built, extending up to George's Meeting.

At the end of October the City Council agreed to the building of a new market and car park in Fore Street, with costs being assisted by a £90 000 payment for war damage.

As 1958 drew to a close one statement referred to the city redevelopment thus: 'Rebuilt Exeter retains its intimacy and human scale. The use of brick is the colour of the Devon landscape.' However, by November 1959 another prominent citizen, solicitor G F S Butt, was calling for the retention of the 226 and 227 High Street stating it would be 'sheer vandalism to destroy the two buildings. They are part of the city's stock in trade'. In this month Exeter's Theatre Royal, too, came under threat of closure.

In early December the ruins of St Catherine's Almshouses in Catherine Street achieved listing as a National Monument. They were tidied up and designated to be used as a haven and resting place for the public.

The finishing touches were carried out to the Inner Bypass in April and May 1959 in time for its opening date of 10 May. An announcement was also made that a second river bridge would be built sometime in the 1960s, at a cost of £450 000 which would complete the scheme. In mid-August the Ministry of Transport refused a second application to close the lower end of Northernhay Street to vehicles, this having been first applied for in 1957. In St Thomas demolition of Cowick Street began, with the intention of creating a dual carriageway to the new Exe Bridge.

October saw the construction of Bailey Street and Musgrave Row under way and No. 17, Husseys the Auctioneers, a Queen Anne building in Gandy Street, was demolished. Work had started on Paris Street in March and in November 1959 it was officially opened, now widened from 20ft to 44ft and with three of the original shops still standing: Bealeys the grocers, Endacott Sellicks, fishing tackle and general dealer, and drapers Smallridges.

Another area of dissension for the City Council in December centred on Eastgate Square which was already under construction, but the chairman of the streets committee stated: 'It is too late for the Council to change its mind as 50 per cent of the work is done. There has been a major blunder at Eastgate.'

The inexorable pressure to remove the city's older buildings continued into 1960 with another application to remove Nos 226 and 227 High Street, first proposed two years earlier. The Minister of Housing and Local Government replied that demolition could not be resisted.

Sidwell Street was in the news in March with a statement that a new shopping centre would be ready for Christmas. A modern market costing £45 000 was nearing completion, comprising 13 small lock-ups with two island kiosks, leading to a central hall. The market building still exists but the frontage has been adapted to take a number of shops. It is centrally located, on the south side of Sidwell Street, just before Summerland Street. Eastgate House, meanwhile, was nearing completion at the top of High Street.

To help to make their stay in the City an enjoyable and interesting one, visitors to Exeter are invited to call at the **INFORMATION BUREAU**, situated in Queen Street, adjacent to the 'Bus Stations.

Here a copy of the Street Plan of the City, a large-scale map covering the whole of Devon, Exeter Directories and various Telephone Directories are available for reference, and the following publications can also be obtained :

Official Guide to the City. Price 1/- (by post, 1/3).

Street Plan in Folder form. Price 6d. (by post, 8d.)

Folder—'A Day in Exeter'. No charge.

An Accommodation List and other literature will be forwarded free on on request, postage 2d.

All enquiries should be addressed to The Secretary, Publicity & Information Bureau, 18 Queen, Street, Exeter. Telephone 2434.

In late April the foundation stone of the new Pannier Market and Corn Exchange (St George's Market) in Fore Street was laid and all the shops let. The Victorian police station in Waterbeer Street was earmarked for removal, and it was stated that the Roman pavement in the foyer would be preserved. It was removed and preserved for ten years in the Royal Albert Memorial Museum but later destroyed in error. The police station had closed in 1959 after seventy-three years on the site.

Later that month the public learned of the formation of a new body, the Exeter Group, dedicated to preserving the historic atmosphere of the past and to promoting the new amenities. The brainchild of Professor Hoskins, the historian, the group later became the Exeter Civic Society. At the society's inaugural public meeting on 17 March 1961 at St Luke's College, it was ruefully suggested that the Society had been formed ten years too late and should have been in existence at the very start of rebuilding. The role of the Society, however, would be to 'stimulate civic pride, cultivate an informed awareness, encourage good taste and informed comment'.

In June further criticism was expressed by the principal of Exeter College of Art regarding the disappointing way in which the city was taking shape. He suggested a small Commission should be set up to combine the best of old and new. 'Something has to be done,' he stated.

In August 1960 news was released of a new project for Paris Street, instigated by the owners, the Church Commissioners. The city's biggest single scheme to date, it was to extend from the corner of Paris Street up to Bampfylde Street, and would be contemporary in design but intended to blend with older-style properties. A special feature would be created at the corner of Paris Street in the shape of a round shop unit.

The postwar future for the remaining lower Sidwell Street properties was total destruction and the bold claim was that 'new life' would be brought to 'the street that died'.

One month later it was announced that the terrace of cottages in Commercial Road, overlooking the leat, would be demolished at some future date and that the whole area was up for development. At the same time, the Northam Foundry, occupied by Colletts, was also being obliterated. Early in 1961 freelance writer and historian Jacqueline Warren wrote about the level of destruction occurring in the city, titled 'Enterprise Destruction'. The area of Exe Island and New Bridge Street was now earmarked for major changes. It was recommended that a new bridge should replace the original archway created as part of the New Bridge Street Viaduct in 1774; this delightful entrance joined Frog Street with Exe Island. The Mission buildings and other interesting properties adjacent to the archway would also be bulldozed. It was the beginning of the end of an era for Exe Island.

In late October 1960 Exeter was hit by some of the worst floods in its history with, worse still, a repetition in December. Millions of gallons of water poured down the Exe, overflowing into St Thomas, affecting hundreds of houses and causing serious damage to many premises. The severity of the situation was to lead to the instigation of a major flood prevention scheme to protect the city. This was to extend from Cowley Weir to Countess Wear and was undertaken from 1965 to 1977, bringing about fundamental changes to the riverside. It has proved a huge success to date.

The year 1961 was a busy time for Sidwell Street as the new market had opened and it was announced that a seven-storey block could be built for retail company Bobby's at Eastgate, on the corner of Longbrook Street and Sidwell Street, today occupied by Debenhams. All properties adjoining the site on the north side were to be removed. Much of what had been familiar to Exeter residents in Sidwell Street disappeared. In August it was suggested that the new St George's Market would be ready for the following Easter. Work had started in August 1959 and it had been constructed on the site of the previously blitzed market.

In September the City Council accepted the proposals for the new bus station at Paris Street.

An interesting situation happened in November 1961 when Associated British Cinemas formally objected to a kiosk newly erected opposite the Savoy Cinema at the top of High Street. It was branded as 'an eyesore and obscures the canopy of the cinema that has recently been erected and blocks the public view'. This small structure was to draw very strong comments from the public but the request for its removal was denied and it continued to trade as a tobacconist.

In November there was great excitement as the project to move No. 16 Edmund Street got under way. On 5 December it was announced that 'the house will be moved tomorrow'. It would be taken from its original site, where it had stood for over 500 years, to a new site in West Street but this did not transpire until 11 December. It created international headlines as 'The House That Moved'. Another historic site was also in the news, at St Peter's Corner, the junction of North Street with High Street. Owing to a shop refurbishment the famous medieval statue of St Peter was taken down and repainted in red, blue and gold. It was later returned to its alcove on the front of the building at the top of North Street but is now in the Royal Albert Memorial Museum.

A new scheme to protect Exeter from flooding was also making news. The project would involve the building of two massive tunnels constructed to run underneath the city, taking water out into the lower estuary flood plain. The project failed to gain support.

In February 1962 the outrageous proposal to destroy some of Exeter's prime historic buildings in High Street again hit the headlines. Professor Hoskins, as chairman of the Civic Society, expressed the view that the buildings could be saved and there were suggestions that both buildings could be moved. It was not until January 1969 that it was finally announced that the whole corner site would remain. However, only the historic sixteenth- and seventeenth-century frontages of Nos 226 and 227 were retained. In the early 1970s the interiors were demolished, along with the ground-floor shop fronts. The façades were to be supported by using upright steel girders at ground level and not integrated into the new rear buildings.

At this time the face of St Thomas was also changing as the corner of Cowick Street was removed and traffic redirected around a newly constructed roundabout.

In March the biggest plan yet for the rebuilding of Exeter's city centre was shown. It would involve High Street, Queen Street, North Street and Paul Street and the proposed demolition of the nineteenth-century Higher Market, also in Queen Street. The concept would transform the area into a pedestrian precinct. One month later the plan was referred back to the planning committee with the comment that the project required more thought. It would cost £1 075 000 and involve a major new traffic route. Within days a London company announced a grand plan for the site that would involve a new Civic Hall, hotel with 100 rooms, department store and a piazza.

The development of Exeter provided plenty of fodder not only for local newspapers but the nationals too. An article in the *Guardian* in May 1962 was headlined 'Exeter Phoenix a sorry bird – Opportunity wasted in rebuilding'. The new style of architecture was referred to as 'uniformly dressed in a bombastic, bastardised sort of suburban Georgian with the criterion being the rateable value'.

Five months later, in September, a further scheme was put forward by an insurance company, at a cost of £5 million and designed to redevelop 'The Golden Heart of Exeter'.

One month later a public display was shown at Hughes' garage in Princesshay by the newly formed Exeter Central Traders Association. Three schemes had been prepared by the Association who had worked in conjunction with planning consultants. The redevelopment of the central area was to prove a highly controversial project. In early February 1963 two more schemes were put forward, followed by a statement from the Council: 'We are getting more confused.' Attendance had been poor at city centre debates and in July the City Council announced they would seek 'independent advice'. In mid-July all seven proposals were discussed. The situation was to remain unresolved until ten years later in 1973 when the scheme by developers Laing was finally passed by the City Council.

In June of that year buildings in Sidwell Street were being demolished to make way for Bobby's new store, the drawings having been released in February.

Altogether 1963 was to be a highly contentious period, as the plan for a new central area road was also launched. It was to be the subject of a hot debate and opposed by Professor Hoskins who was a Liberal councillor. Numerous letters were published in the press in 1964, with serious friction developing directly involving individual councillors including Professor Hoskins. It created an unprecedented situation.

The focus shifted to the River Exe in June, with plans for the two new bridges and the removal of the early-twentieth-century bridge.

By mid-November Professor Hoskins was once again in the news stating: 'The postwar rebuilding of Exeter is a disaster. It might look well in an outer London suburb.'

In October 1964 a new start was made on developing a plan for the Guildhall area with the engagement of planning consultants for a Town Centre Map. This was followed in November 1966 by the recommendation: 'Do not pull down the Civic Hall or Higher Market.' The Civic Hall was duly demolished but the façade and central hall of the Higher Market retained.

At the beginning of July 1967 a plan was announced for creation of new Civic Offices at Dix's Field, with work scheduled to start in September 1968, at a cost of £1 160 000. The buildings had none of the former style and elegance of the historic site on which they stood. The remaining period houses on the east side of Dix's Field were demolished to allow construction and prefabricated buildings erected. The Civic Centre was later nicknamed 'the egg box'.

In December 1967 the Council's planning committee increased its grants from £500 to £2000 to save the city's older buildings, stating that it would keep watch on interesting buildings following letters from the public. At the same time Mount Pleasant Methodist Church was demolished to be replaced by flats.

In January 1970 a controversial building was being erected on Exe Island, confronting drivers and pedestrians coming over Exe Bridge. The multi-storeyed Renslade House has found great disfavour over the years and was elected at one time as one of Exeter's most ugly buildings. Renslade House was completed in mid-August 1971 and was heavily criticised as being 'a blot on the landscape' and 'a tragic development from Exeter City Council members'.

Cowick Street, meanwhile, was being evacuated in preparation for the new road scheme leading up to Exe Bridge.

Early in 1971 the disused Victorian church Mary Major was demolished in Cathedral Yard. An archaeological dig uncovered a Saxon Minster and, underneath, the remains of the largest Roman military bathhouse in the country. Despite plans to exhibit the site as an attraction, it was covered over and in 2003 still awaits an opportunity to exploit it.

In early March 1971, at Queen Street corner, the east side Victorian buildings were razed to the ground and another controversy boiled over with the construction of the new C & A store. The original sympathetic nineteenth-century buildings were replaced by a controversial brick structure. It was a devastating indictment of the failure to recognise the importance of one of Exeter's most sensitive sites, and created a public outcry. In April a petition was started against the proposed design.

In Paris Street Phase One of the Civic Centre had been completed. There was 'no official opening, no champagne lunch just a businesslike move', with Phase Two still under construction. Five phases had been planned originally. The City Council moved from Southernhay West, its base since 1897. A description of the new building started with: 'It should harmonise easily with the existing historic styles,' the scheme being passed by the Fine Arts Commission in 1967.

In July the area of Newtown was highlighted when a huge plan was announced to give a facelift to the city's 'twilight area'. A combination of war damage and older properties had left the area needing considerable modernisation. This particular project has worked extremely well, retaining the character of the area, the community and improving living conditions.

In June 1972 a £1 million scheme was put forward by the Sun Alliance & London Insurance Group, to redevelop the top of Southernhay. The site had been used as a car park following the destruction of the period Regency terraces in 1942. The resulting project consists of a massive brick edifice bearing little resemblance to former buildings. Its dominating presence jars against its refined neighbours.

In March of that year attention was drawn to No. 38 North Street, a fine seventeenth-century building that was at risk owing to the proposed Guildhall development scheme, but the building was nevertheless destroyed.

In late March the newly excavated Roman bathhouse aroused the interest of expert archaeologists who come to the city to view the remains.

Another historic feature was also to be in the news in January 1973 when the ferry service at Exeter Quay was threatened with closure. The City Council had a statutory obligation to operate the service but was seeking to relinquish the responsibility. An insurance broker, Mr George Butt, fought for its retention, organising a public petition which was signed by 66 residents and 2500 visitors. Together they succeeded in saving the service after a seven-hour inquiry.

The Guildhall development was in the news in July 1973. The detailed plans showing the Paul Street elevation were heavily criticised, with some council members referring to it as 'like a barracks block', but the plans were approved. The City Architect commented: 'The overall design right round is going to knit into a nice homogeneous building.' Today Paul Street is recognised as one of the most characterless roads in central Exeter!

In September of the same year the Council put forward a £1.5 million plan for the junction of Holloway Street that would radically change the area. A major factor was a road that would run through Bull Meadow Park. It created a huge outcry from local residents, with result that the road change was dropped.

In late November 1973 a rare archaeological find was discovered in a pit, during excavations at the corner of Paul Street and North Street. An almost complete 5¼-inch statue of a Celtic Venus was found and taken to the Royal Albert

Memorial Museum. A few days later the priceless object was filmed for a television news item at the museum, but when the work had been completed the statue mysteriously disappeared. Despite major efforts by the museum the object was never recovered.

In April 1974 the Exeter Information Bureau, which had occupied a site on the corner of Queen Street and Paul Street, moved to the new Civic Centre in Paris Street. Their rustic timber-framed building was demolished. In June a new Processional Way was proposed for the Cathedral Close, and a no-parking policy was later agreed on 3 February 1975.

On 17 February 1975 publicity was given to the selling of the Tudor House in Tudor Street. The early-seventeenth-century building had been painstakingly restored by Mr Bill Lovell over a twelve-year period. He approached the City Council in the hope that it could be retained as a tourist attraction and become a prominent part of the city's heritage. His proposal was turned down and the property was put on the open market at a cost of £60 000.

The area of South Street and Magdalen Street made news in December 1975, with an announcement that a Development Brief was being instigated for developers. This would inform them that the area contained a number of listed buildings and that any design would have to be sympathetic. The final scheme for the area eradicated nearly all existing buildings.

The new £5 million shopping centre, named 'The Golden Heart Project', was exposed to the public for the first time when the hoardings came down in August 1976. The first large store to open was Littlewoods, followed by more in September when the project was officially opened by Princess Alexandra.

One month later the public were informed that there was a good chance that Marks & Spencer would develop the site of Waltons in High Street. The company was reported be in agreement with the reconstruction of historic façades but would not retain listed shop fronts.

In June 1977 Magdalen Street was struggling for survival with reports stating: 'City terrace that died of vandalism'. The failure to protect historic properties had left them in appalling condition and near the point of falling down. Yet the listed buildings had been acknowledged as 'structurally sound' in 1975. The City Council was criticised for their lack of attention and dragging their feet and making no attempt to save them.

One month later the whole of the street was demolished.

During this month shoppers were asked why they came to Exeter. Favourable replies quoted 'better shops, convenience and car park facilities'. Of people interviewed, 25 per cent liked being undercover and found that it was easier when accompanied by children. A minority stated the new city centre was dull, unimaginative, clinical and uninspired.

The townscape of Bartholomew Street was to be the focus of the Civic Society in October, putting forward a plan to protect the historic townscape that was falling into disrepair. The Society stated that the area 'must not go the same way as Magdalen Street', as there was no coherent policy for restoration of the surrounding area.

In April 1979 it was stated that St Petrock's Church was no longer needed and that ideas for its future use were required. Also in this month the new Marks & Spencer store was being built.

In the later part of the year, in October, the new residential development of Shilhay became newsworthy with the headline: 'City's Colditz wins design prize'. The competition was sponsored by the Secretary of State for the Environment and the IRBA. It was stated that the controversial City Council Project was 'well designed and successfully relates to the existing area'.

Peter Thomas
Exeter 2003

A City in Ruins – the State of Play

The bombing of Exeter on 4 May 1942 left much of the city devastated in a raid that lasted just one hour. Some of the city's historic buildings still stood but were gutted. In High Street the façades of the General Post Office at Eastgate, St Lawrence Church, the Commercial Union and Lloyds Bank, together with Dellers Café, still remained but were later demolished.

The central area of Exeter is seen from South Street, bottom, to Sidwell Street. Wartime destruction devastated the central area including High Street, Bedford [illegible]eet, Catherine Street, Bampfylde Street, Southernhay East, Paris Street, Sidwell Street, South Street an[illegible]reet. Damage also occurred to some outlying areas. Approximately 10 000 incendiary bombs and 16[illegible] ons of high explosives were dropped on the city.

The most significant postwar Exeter photo, shown here, records the High Street after the demolition of remaining standing buildings, with the exception of the National Westminster Bank at Castle Street and Barclays Bank at Bedford Street. On the oval site of Bedford Circus, top left, the trees in the central garden have escaped destruction. Behind, the gutted shell of Bedford Chapel still stands.

A view from Catherine Street to the Cathedral shows part of the destroyed site of Bedford Circus in Bedford Street.

Shown from its west side is the gutted ruin of the Chapel at Bedford Circus. Beyond is the decimated central area, c.*1943.*

" SOUTH-WEST METROPOLIS "

Sir,—Cit's observations on post-war expenditure are a timely reminder of a truth which some of us are apt to overlook in our zeal for large-scale civic re-planning.

However, the widespread interest evinced, and expressed in the columns of your newspaper and in one's personal contacts, is a happy augury of a popular welcome to proposals for a broad-based and Statesmanlike scheme of civic reconstruction. It is axiomatic that a bold and comprehensive scheme of civic rehabilitation and expansion is the sole foundation on which we can hope to build a civic economy capable of re-absorbing and maintaining a population of pre-war dimensions.

But, as Cit so aptly implies, nothing that is worth while is achieved without effort, and he does well to call attention to a fact that cannot be too often or too strongly emphasised, namely, that the re-establishment of the city as the metropolis of the South-west can be accomplished only at the cost of a grievous burden of rate expenditure over a long period of years.

It would be well for our citizens to be in no doubt of that incontrovertible truth.

A.G.W.

One of two views showing the remains of Bedford Circus after demolition and clearance. The spire of St Mary Major Church is shown centre, and Bedford Chapel on the right.

Bedford Chapel is shown with the central oval garden of Bedford Circus. Cars still continued to park on the remaining road around the garden.

An early-postwar photo, c.*1943, shows large billboards along the cleared High Street. It appears that large-scale posters depicitng wartime scenes of soldiers in action, may have been used for propaganda. The largest poster displayed a figure of £760 000 and a title 'Will they fall there now'.*

South Street and its adjacent streets had been subjected to such a high level of bombing that total clearance of the area was necessary. The side streets, bearing ancient names, were to be obliterated, opening up new vistas. At the top of South Street medieval buildings that had been hidden from view by the destroyed Globe Hotel emerged into view for the first time. The ruin shown right is the Hall of the Vicars Choral.

The clearance of South Street, bottom, on its west side, gave a clear view not only of the Haldon Hills but of Follett Buildings and Mermaid Yard, top left. Random dwarf walls contained the rubble in the area. The central thoroughfare shown was Sun Street, leading to Preston Street.

The clearance of upper South Street exposed the rear of the Lower Market, the substantial structure of which, built from huge granite blocks, was to remain for some years. The Italianate-style building was unique in Exeter. The prominent central building with chimney was Evans Gadd, Wholesale Druggists, who occupied Nos 6 to 11 Smythen Street. Their 1920s warehouse remained until very recent times. The site has now been taken over for housing.

In 1945 Town Planner Thomas Sharp was asked by the City Council to draw up plans for the city's redevelopment. In 1946 a Public Inquiry was held in the Guildhall, seen here, relating to the acquisition of land by compulsory purchase. Despite concerns of local traders about the potential loss of valuable freehold sites in the city, the Council was to gain the powers of compulsory purchase and the task was of rebuilding began.

The City Council was to employ a new Planning Officer, Mr Harold Gayton, in 1946. He was to steer Exeter through most of its postwar redevelopment, having already worked in the City Engineers Department of the City Council. Mr Gayton who retired in 1974 worked hand in hand with Thomas Sharp.

The End of Hostilities – Time to Celebrate!

On 8 May 1945 Exeter held its VE Day (Allied Victory in Europe) celebrations. As elsewhere in Britain residents organised street parties, with trestle tables laden with long-awaited treats, as seen here in Pamela Road. Mums, dads, grand-parents, neighbours and children alike joined in the festivities across the city.

Union Jacks flutter in among a mountain of cakes, buns and other delicious goodies, served up to the children of Pamela Road. Among those watching over the celebrations is Mr E Hopkins, a well-known science teacher from Episcopal School, seen far right.

In Exwick, families came together and celebrated all day, with accordion music to accompany the jolly proceedings.

On VJ Day (Allied Victory over Japan) 15 August 1945 Exeter's floodlit High Street filled with hundreds of people of all ages to dance the night away. This scene is outside Colsons' department store.

On 2 June 1953 tables were laid out in Toronto Road for a street party to celebrate the coronation of Queen Elizabeth II.

The New-look Exeter

The postwar period was to change the face of central Exeter. It was time for new ideas, concepts and architecture. In reality the completed city centre would have little bearing on its previous character. Central High Street is shown with the uniform block design that was to predominate. The street was to be widened by 50 per cent, creating wider pavements and initially two-way traffic continued. The age of the department store was still to come to Exeter.

Building was to start first on the north side of High Street, and it is interesting to note that the concept for coal fires had not diminished, as the architect's drawing shows smoke rising from a line of chimneys that were part of the design. Not all aspects of proposed details shown in drawings took place.

The postwar corner of High Street and Castle Street was to bear no comparison to its pre-war narrow junction that only allowed one vehicle at a time access to Castle Street. There had been some interesting pre-war High Street properties next to this site, including the Empire Cinema and, on the opposite corner, Charles's shoe shop. The new concept at this point was to open the area into a small square, and today this offers a welcome break from a line of similar shop fronts.

In High Street the well-known store of Colsons was to change its image totally by the addition of a further building adjacent to St Stephen's Church, left. Although part of the old decorative shop front remained it was eventually removed. The new building was to incorporate a new feature – a long concrete undercover front canopy to protect customers from adverse weather conditions. Shown right is the historic building occupied by Barratts' shoe shop,which was later removed.

The new building adjacent to St Stephen's Church was to be bookseller Wyman & Son. It was to be created from what was latterly the arcade of Bobby's who also had owned a prominent property on the other side of the church. The arcade extended from High Street around the back of the church, joining with St Stephen's Street and the famous bow. The entry leading to Catherine Street was to be retained. The old front of Colsons is shown in this drawing.

READERS' LETTERS

'Plans For City's Prestige'

Sir,—Messrs. Bruford's arguments re the future Exeter are at variance one with the other. With their remarks re the recapture of the city's pre-war trade and, if possible, increasing the volume of same, everyone will agree, as this will redound to our mutual advantage.

The retention of the High-street in its pre-war condition of traffic congestion and narrow side walks on the grounds of a narrow thoroughfare being preferable to a wide one as a shopping centre may be correct.

The next argument is at variance with this, as it is suggested that, in order to avoid congestion and facilitate the business of shopping, a by-pass road be constructed. Should this suggestion be implemented it will have the effect of turning potential customers away from the city's shopping centre, to our mutual disadvantage.

Here are some ideas for our post-war city:—Clear the whole of the area, Paris-street—South-street, inclusive of Southernhay and Bedford Circus. In the centre of this cleared space would be erected our new civic buildings (mediaeval or modern architecture). Built in a circle round this would be an arcade of business premises and shops to house our leading business firms, banks and insurance coys. This arcade would be inclusive of the Cathedral, with Close, the Guildhall, with, perhaps, "The Express and Echo" and Ross buildings for their mediaeval characteristics, so little of which is left to the city following the blitz. Radiating from the arcade would be wide boulevards, giving access to the environs of the city. Also, the adoption of the suggestion for the provision of a car park under Northernhay, with the construction of an all services 'bus depot over the Central Station. The Cathedral Close to be retained as it is at present. With the whole of the buildings appertaining to the Cathedral renovated this would provide a secluded and quiet rest centre for visitors as well as retaining the old-world atmosphere which emanates from proximity to this ancient edifice. Fore-street and Bridge-street, reconstructed as a wide boulevard, would provide visitors with a grand view over Haldon, a vista of great beauty; the banks of the Exe, laid out as promenade gardens from Port Royal to the Flower Pot. These improvements would raise the prestige of the city, making it a fine capital of a lovely county. This plan embodies the views expressed in the letters received by our Editor from men and women now serving with the armed Forces, and who, we all trust, will soon be with us again.

W. LODGE.

7, Bloomfield-terrace, St. James, Exeter.

The rear of Colsons and Wymans, together with St Stephen's Church, was used to form the sides of a square and was to be landscaped. Underground public conveniences, with a flower bed at street level, replaced those previously situated in Bedford Street outside Dellers Café.

The junction of Bedford Street with Catherine Street was completely redesigned. The site of the Devon & Exeter Savings Bank, which was totally destroyed in the blitz, was to be used for a spacious four-storey building for Martins Bank. The entry into Catherine Street was made far wider.

Wartime damage was to be tastefully restored in Southernhay East, with an excellent reconstruction of the Regency Terrace. Unfortunately this practice was not common in postwar Exeter.

Plan To Solve Traffic Problem And

KEEP OLD EXETER

TAKING the view that "for various good reasons" the future of High-street "will be no wider than it is at present," and that this will mean that "in a short time after the resumption of peacetime motoring traffic will be impossible" in that thoroughfare, Mr. E. C. Cole, of 26, Summerway, Whipton, sets out in a letter a plan for helping to preserve as much of the old Exeter as possible."

In the postwar period many schemes were put forward but perhaps one of the most startling was the idea of demolishing nearly every building in Queen Street, Paul Street, North Street and the ancient part of High Street. It left the Guildhall as an isolated structure integrated into a modern building. This horrendous project came very near to succeeding.

Postwar Aerial Views

Right: *The elegant central location of Dix's Field had received severe damage to its nineteenth-century terraces on the west and east side, with many buildings being gutted. Properties still existed intact on both sides but only the end buildings on the west side were to be retained and restored. The east side was to become the site for the new Civic Centre which resulted in the removal of its remaining standing buildings. Photo c.1955.*

Below: *Trinity Street leading from South Street to Southernhay West followed the line of the City Wall. Small warehouses and cottages existed in the street, along with a group of small industrial buildings, of which one housed the city's Sheriff's Coach. The site opposite the old Royal Devon & Exeter Hospital, bottom centre, was previously Trinity Graveyard. Today the street is a landscaped City Wall walkway and most of the area is taken up by the South Gate Hotel and its car park.*

Above: *Southernhay West, classed as some of the finest properties in Exeter, received some bomb damage to buildings on the south side, centre left, but were to be sensitively rebuilt. The work retained the proportions and dignity of the original Regency Terraces which had extensive rear gardens. Barnfield Road and the Barnfield Theatre are seen right.*

Left: *The immediate postwar period was a time to rectify severe damage to some of the city's most historic properties. The almost total destruction of the medieval properties, Nos 11 and 12 The Close, left only the wall facing The Close standing, with, remarkably, the two stone entrances intact. The properties had backed on to an Elizabethan building called the Abbot's Lodge that was destroyed by a high-explosive bomb. A restoration programme was instigated and the buildings reconstructed. Today it is hard to distinguish where the old finishes and the new begins.*

The area from High Street to Paul Street was a tightly-knit townscape that had evolved over a long period of time. The back street, Waterbeer Street, was the site of a large foundry belonging to ironmongers Garton & King and in the same street stood the prominent Victorian police station. The north side of Paul Street had become the bus and coach station and is clearly seen as an open space. Postwar development saw the removal of the majority of buildings in this central area and, with them, its former character.

A detailed view of Waterbeer Street shows the Victorian police station with its prominent decorative chimney. All the buildings on the north side of the street were to be removed, with the site eventually being developed as the Guildhall Shopping Centre. At the rear is shown the extensive frontage and roofline of the Higher Market and Civic Hall.

Exeter's second market, the Lower Market in Fore Street, was an important architectural feature but was subject to severe wartime damage. The shell of the building remained until the early-60s but was finally demolished. It was replaced by St George's Hall.

The junction of South Street, Magdalen Street and Holloway Street was a community in its own right with a number of interesting and important period properties. It had a high density of housing, alleyways and courtyards and importantly had evolved around the site of the old South Gate. The whole of the area was to be removed following the decision to create the Western Way Inner Bypass. The notable terrace of properties in Magdalen Street became the site of the Forte Hotel in 1987. The curving lower properties are Friars Walk.

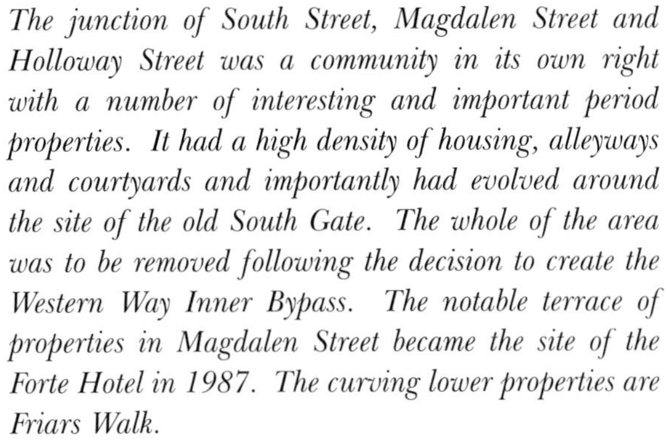

The south side of the city has, through the centuries, retained a significant stretch of the City Wall. Its retention was assisted by the building of properties against and up to the ancient fabric. An almost hidden small lane, called Quay Lane, led the visitor to a unique area where a row of nineteenth-century cottages and other early dwellings led down to the Quay. Cottage gardens backed up to the City Wall. In the 1960s the whole area was demolished, including a section of the ancient City Wall.

The area of the city to the west, referred to by locals as the West Quarter, housed many of Exeter's workers and to assist in the education of the young a school was built in 1850 that overlooked Coombe Street, seen right. Central School became a focal point of the community. Adjacent to the school, accommodation was also built in the form of large tenements that housed poorer families. Follett Buildings and Central School were demolished in the late-1970s to make way for new housing. Photo c.*1955.*

Coombe Street, an ancient thoroughfare leading towards Exeter Quay, was created in a natural shallow valley or combe and bordered by the City Wall on the south side. In the early-postwar period the street still retained a number of three-storeyed nineteenth-century houses with courtyards. In 1927 the City Wall collapsed on the Custom House Inn at the bottom of Quay Lane, necessitating its demolition. The crumbled wall is seen bottom centre.

For many people living on the west side of the city their workplace would have been in the area of the Quay and Shilhay. This record shows Exeter's riverside as it will never be seen again. The high-density industrial area of Shilhay was to be swept away for new housing and for the implementation of a new flood prevention scheme after the severe flooding of 1960.

The River Exe and Exeter Ship Canal were primary factors contributing to Exeter's wealth during the sixteenth to nineteenth centuries. The canal is seen entering the River Exe and at this junction is the Basin, constructed in 1830. The new facility allowed greater ease of mooring and transportation via a railway branch line. Exeter Gasworks and Willeys Ironfounders & Gas Appliance Manufacturers, were at one time the city's largest employers. The whole of this area was to be converted into new houses and apartments during the 80s and 90s.

Aerial view of Exeter, 1960.

The area shown is the outskirts of Exeter at Alphington. It shows the land that was due to become Marsh Barton Trading Estate. Shown bottom is the railway line and the original railway bridge that crossed over Alphington Road. The circular area off centre is the first Exeter Speedway Track. In the postwar period a vast proportion of this land was used for industrial purposes. Photo c.*1945.*

Sidwell Street is shown before the rebuilding of the south side between Summerland Street and Belmont Road. The construction of the Inner Bypass is shown crossing the central area and new industrial premises.

Reviving Business – Temporary Shops

In 1947 it was decided that to help trading to return to the city centre, temporary shops, with a limited lifespan of perhaps fifteen years, should be built. The sites designated for the project were at Eastgate adjacent to the Cooperative Society building and would extend down Southernhay East, a section of road that no longer exists. The buildings were simple single-storey units of precast concrete. The start of building is shown Southernhay East.

This view looks from the East Angle Bastion of the City Wall towards High Street. It shows the new temporary shops being completed. A section of the City Wall had extended across the top of Princesshay but was demolished to allow completion of the new pedestrian project. The Bastion still stands at the corner of Post Office Street.

The new complex of L-shaped temporary shops extended from High Street towards Southernhay, turning towards Paris Street. An area for car parking was created between the Cooperative Society and the rear of the shops. Photo c.1953.

The flat-roofed precast shops erected at Eastgate were to house over 20 retailers, allowing shopping to once again take place in the central area. Shops fronting Princesshay in this early-1950s' record include Ann, milliner Luscombes, drapers, Edith Waldon, skirts, John's, teas, Frank White, optician, Arthur Hunt, baker, Typewriter Technicians, Michaels, furriers, Chandler, photographers, Randall, shoes, Mayne, knitwear, Eastgate Post Office, Melhuish, furnishers, Windsor, tailor, Joan Frazer, gowns, Bennetts, tailors, Ellams, duplicators, and Mansell, chemists. The remains of the City Wall have been demolished and the site changed to accommodate two stone-walled gardens.

This photo taken from High Street towards Southernhay across the top of Princesshay shows the temporary post-war shops, left, and, behind, the spire of Southernhay Congregational Church. The advertising boards, centre, are for Hughes' multi-storey garage, construction of which is about to begin. The new High Street premises of Wolfe & Hollander Ltd, furnishers, advertises '2000 yards of lined linoleum at 6/11 a square yard'!

The view towards High Street from the temporary shops at Eastgate, c.1955. The building beyond, central left, is the rebuilt end of Northernhay Place. Building work had not started on this section of High Street at this time leaving Northernhay Place still exposed. The open High Street site was used for car parking.

F C Perry, hairdresser, at temporary shops, Eastgate.

Rebuilding of Colsons

The well known pre-war High Street department store of Colsons (now Dingles) had a long history stretching back to 1792 and was one of the oldest stores in the West Country. The premises abutted Barratts and Bobby's Arcade, adjacent to St Stephen's Church. The premises were badly damaged during the raid on 4 May 1942 by a concentration of incendiary bombs and the blast from a high-explosive bomb nearby. Fire fighters fought to save the building that had been partially gutted. Integrated into the rear of the property had been a 4ft 6 inch cob wall that saved the building from total destruction. In this photo the large display windows are decorated for Christmas and the restaurant is advertised. In 1925 the company was sold to Bright's of Bournemouth but the Colson name was retained.

Colsons' site was to be completely re-developed, with the east side, next to the church, being built first. It was however, to house a new Wymans' book shop. The photograph is taken from the site of the former Commercial Union building after its demolition.

The building for Colsons was to have a new entrance, seen centre, with a concrete canopy. The east side is shown nearing completion and awaiting the insertion of windows, manufactured by Hopes. The west side still retains the original decorated nineteenth-century façade of the old store that also includes a false bow-fronted window.

The new building in High Street required a quantity of steel girders and these were delivered by lorry and lifted into the site by hand. Here, a girder is stretched across High Street.

Barratts of Northampton were to take over 37 High Street adjacent to Colsons. Previously the building had been occupied by bakers Palmer & Edwards. The word 'café' still appears on the façade. The double-gabled seventeenth-century building, was declared as 'unsafe' and demolished. Its bow-fronted neighbour was, more than likely, false.

Barratts' site at 37 High Street, looking through Catherine Street after its removal. The Midland Bank is next door with its windows braced with timber. Scaffolding is provided by SGB of Exeter and the architects and surveyors for the new building are Jerman & Radford of New North Road.

As with many buildings in Exeter it was often necessary to fill in old cellars and to create new foundations. A steel girder was lifted by chains on to the site to create the skeleton of the new building. The chemists Timothy Whites & Taylors can be seen on the corner of High Street and Gandy Street.

Decorated frontages, as seen at Colson & Co., as it was then known, would no longer be seen in Exeter and the remains of the old building was torn down. The adjacent site of Barratts was to have new foundations and eventually helped to create a completely new look for this section of High Street.

The east side of Colsons was initially to be two shops, Wymans and Modelia. These units were to be taken over by Colsons at a later date, creating the store we know today as Dingles. The new entrance canopy of Colsons was planted with flowers and flower tubs fixed on the lamppost. Floral features were to proliferate in the post- war period. A large contractors' board states: General Contractors M T Sleeman & Sons – Architects F W Beech & E Curnow Cooke, Dix's Field.

Below: *Colsons' High Street entrance.*

The rebuilt site in High Street for Colsons, Barratts and Wymans. A uniform style of architecture was to predominate in the new central area of Exeter

The design for the rear of Colsons was to include a rounded corner entrance into Catherine Street. The photo is taken from the site opposite being used to construct a garage for H E Williams, motor engineers.

H E Williams, motor engineers, Catherine Street c.1955. The garage was later removed and a new retail complex of four shops erected.

The rear of Colsons was decorated for the opening of the store.

Colsons' new furniture showroom, selling Stag furniture.

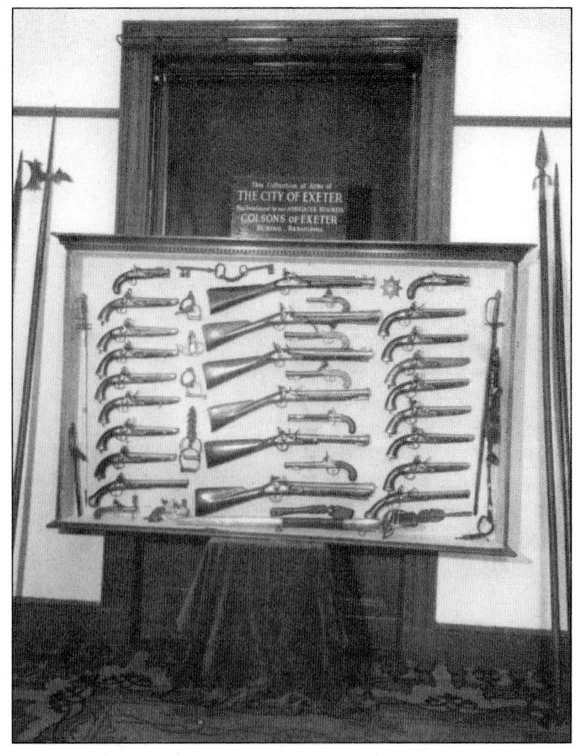

During the rebuilding a special display was mounted of a Collection of Arms of the City of Exeter.

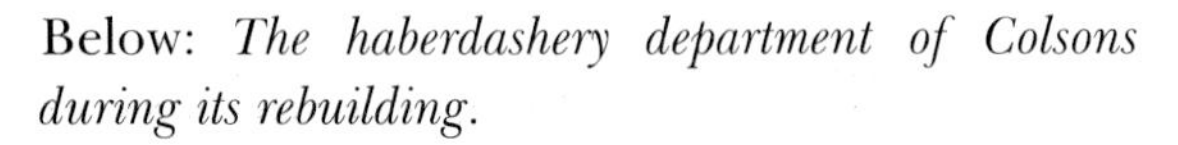

Below: *The haberdashery department of Colsons during its rebuilding.*

Colsons' new restaurant.

The gown showroom.

Exeter's first escalator.

The hat department.

Girls' clothing department.

The newly designed postwar shop fronts showed distinct uniformity in design.

Wymans and Modelia fashions are shown finished and trading.

The new shop layout of Wymans had a library on the first floor and fluorescent lights, by now used extensively.

Management and staff at the opening of Wymans.

WYMAN & SONS

30 HIGH STREET, EXETER

For . . .

ALL

MAPS

GUIDES

VIEW CARDS

FOUNTAIN PENS

BOOKS

HOLIDAY REQUISITES & FANCY GOODS

AGENTS FOR **ALL** BOOK CLUBS

Your Newsagent, Stationer & Bookseller whilst you are in Exeter

The library, Wymans, High Street Exeter.

Restoration in Cathedral Close

The Elizabethan building known as the Abbot's Lodge stood at the rear of Nos 11 and 12 Cathedral Close, adjacent to the Cathedral School. The Lodge was destroyed, with loss of life, by a high-explosive bomb in April 1942. The Cathedral School was seriously damaged and later pulled down. Nos 11 and 12, standing at the far south end of the Close, were also destroyed leaving only a small section of front wall containing an ancient archway that faced the Cathedral Yard. Photo c.1956.

The site of Nos 11 and 12 Cathedral Close was cleared in November 1956, leaving a medieval fireplace on an adjoining wall clearly exposed. As with many medieval buildings in the Close and town, the construction of these buildings was red Heavitree sandstone. All original stone was retained and reused for the restoration of the properties. Photo c.1956.

In 1953 the Church Commissioners instigated the restoration of Nos 11 and 12 Cathedral Close. The contractors were Wakeham & Tucker of Whipton and the architect John V Wakeham. The agent was Clutton of Westminster and Quantity Surveyors Randall, Vining & Saunders of Northernhay Place, Exeter. The style of the buildings would follow the original design, utilising Heavitree stone to face brick-built internal walls. Photo 1956.

Careful reconstruction aimed to marry the old with the new, as with the wooden bay window in the photograph, which was not part of the original design. Luckily, the most famous doorway in the Close, at No. 10, narrowly missed destruction and is the most well-known historic door in the city, dating back to 1600. The coat of arms of Bishop Cotton can just be seen above the scaffolding. Photo December 1956.

A view from the rear of Nos 11 and 12 the Close towards the Cathedral, showing the buildings nearing roof level in early 1957.

The rebuilt properties in Cathedral Close, after being tiled. Photo July 1957.

The south end of the Close, with No. 12 shown completed. Today, most people would not be aware that these buildings were reconstructed and they continue to add to the appeal of Cathedral Close. By careful scrutiny of the roof tiles, you may be able to detect where the old finishes and the new begins. The policy of reconstruction and restoration was, however, not given a priority for many buildings in Exeter during the postwar period with the result that unsuitable architectural designs were often to appear and numerous buildings were demolished.

St Catherine's Almshouses Memorial

The raid of May 1942 virtually destroyed one of Exeter's ancient back streets that led to Cathedral Close. Catherine Street, leading to St Martin's Gate and the Close, contained a diminutive group of almshouses and chapel founded in 1450 by Canon John Stevens for 13 poor men. Built from Heavitree stone, the almshouses were severely damaged but the outer shells still stood.

St Catherine's Almshouses had latterly been occupied and run by the Church Army since 1894. The small complex contained its own chapel whose walls, bell turret and bell survived the blitz. The adjacent ruins, shown with temporary construction workers' huts, were also of an historic nature, being the site of a late-fourteenth-century medieval mansion. It was converted into use for Annuellar Priests in the sixteenth century and finally housed the Country House Inn.

In the later postwar period the site of the almshouses and adjacent site of the Country House Inn were styled as a memorial to those who lost their lives in the blitz of 4 May 1942. Parts of the remaining buildings were taken down and the area around the site laid out as a public amenity in the 1980s. During the work a significant Roman mosaic floor was discovered.

Princesshay

Exeter's new pedestrian shopping mall was to be laid out according to Thomas Sharp's recommendations, its focus being an uninterrupted view of Exeter Cathedral. A feature built to commemorate the start of rebuilding of the city was unveiled on 21 October 1949 by HRH Princess Elizabeth, Duchess of Edinburgh, who named the development 'Princesshay'. Integrated into it was a bronze Datum mark from which the new city development was laid out. At this time the central area was devoid of buildings, allowing plenty of car parking. A shopper reads the newly erected bronze panel on the commemorative feature.

The construction of Princesshay took twelve years to complete, the first section being built at the eastern end. There were six shops facing High Street and six facing into Princesshay. It is shown nearly complete in 1952 with newly laid paving. Occupying shops were (from the left) SPCK, Chain Library, Terry & Co., Wolfe & Hollander and Singer.

The top of Princesshay was initially laid out with dwarf walled gardens that followed the line of the demolished City Wall. The Heavitree stone walls were created from material rescued from destroyed historic buildings. Well-known Bampfylde House, constructed from Heavitree stone, stood just a short distance away until blitzed in 1942.

View to the Cathedral showing top part of east section finished.

FEARIS'
EXETER'S
SUPER-MARKET
SITUATED IN THE NEW SHOPPING CENTRE
PRINCESSHAY
Every kind of **FOOD** *under one Roof*
Licensed for Wine, Spirits, Ales, etc.
REASONABLE PRICES, QUALITY AND SERVICE
Deliveries to all parts — Telephone 75144 5

Construction of Princesshay began with the north corner, followed by the south side. The top section was built on the extensive site of the school yard of the Blue Coat School of St John's which had closed in 1931. In October 1957 a Blue Boy statue was erected at the top of Princesshay to commemorate the school. The south side is having foundations laid for Hughes' garage, and the Craftsmen Cleaners have moved next to SPCK.

Pre-war, Hughes' garage had dominated this area being the size of an aircraft hangar and capable of housing a large number of vehicles. Hughes were to rebuild on the site, maintaining their presence in the early postwar years from a small industrial warehouse in the new Post Office Street. A sign board advertises their new building. At this time buildings have been erected at the lower south side of Princesshay. Photo c.*1955.*

Hughes' premises in Post Office Street adjacent to the City Wall.

The new Princesshay project was to be confined by the City Wall, classified as a National Monument, but the City Council sought powers to remove the East Gate section of the wall in order to complete Princesshay. It was duly demolished but the eastern angle bastion was retained and restored. Temporary shops are shown across the top of the site, with the second section joining the South West Gas Company, right, in Southernhay East. Retailers in these units were Cummings, W H Boon, Maypole, Vera Chambers, Eland, F C Perry, Wippel Bros & Row and Denis Davey Cars.

Princesshay is shown with the north side nearly complete and new paving being laid at the west end. Exonians stroll through their new environment with some reservation. The pedestrian precinct was to be laid out with a central line of lamp-posts aligned on the north tower of the Cathedral. Photo c.1960.

Bedford Street is shown looking towards Paris Street with Southernhay to the right. The City Wall crosses diagonally, with car parking on the opposite side. The upper south side of Princesshay is nearing completion and is to become the site of Hughes' garage. The Post Office is still to be built, bottom right.

The large new showroom built for Hughes of Exeter, the main Ford dealer, is shown nearly complete, together with multi-storey car park, in Princesshay. The building also contained five new shop units. Almost all of the new paving has been finished and modern lampposts have been erected.

Diggers remove old basements during Princesshay construction.

Left: *An unusual aspect of the city centre design was construction of the Princesshay Service Road. The concept would allow the servicing of High Street and Princesshay retailers from the rear of their shops, without difficulty. A massive lined trench was dug to create the service road approximately on the line of old Catherine Street. High Street is seen top left, and Princesshay, right.*

Below: *Exeter's Medieval Underground Passages have been a distinctive feature for centuries. Running underneath the central area the stone-walled tunnels suffered war damage and some sections were destroyed. The postwar period heightened interest in the passages and the opportunities to visit them. Previously entry was through manholes in pavements in various parts of the city. A point of entry, at the top of the Princesshay, was opened in 1960 as a tourist attraction.*

Pre-war, a large stone archway in the grounds of St John's School gave access through the City Wall to Southernhay. Its removal allowed a wider opening to be created, giving access for vehicles. On the site of destroyed terraces in Southernhay, a new car park was built. Today the site is Broadwalk House.

'AWAY WITH SENTIMENT'

Sir,—"Old Exonian" evidently lacks foresight. If he wants old streets in preference to modern highways, then the sooner he builds a wall around Exeter and makes it a museum the better.

We, of the younger generation, cannot live in the past, nor can the past buy us bread and butter. If "Old Exonian" still prefers to live in the past, let him go back to his candles, no water in houses, and bad sanitation. No! We have had enough of sentimentality. It is time we cast aside the men with no foresight and put men into power with foresight.

YOUNGER GENERATION.

CITY PLAN PRAISED.

Sir,—Mr. Sharp is to be congratulated on his thoughtful plans for the re-planning of Exeter.

They could hardly be improved upon, and it is to be hoped the E.C.C. will accept them without undue haggling over an un-needed Civic Hall, etc.

RATEPAYER.

Mount Radford, Exeter.

The Southernhay Car Park was to be bordered with flower beds walled with Heavitree stone, this being instigated by City Engineer Mr John Brierley. This concept was the first step towards Exeter establishing its reputation as a 'floral' city.

The opening up of the City Wall allowed excavations by archaeologist Lady Aileen Fox. Her work revealed that the City Wall at this point in Post Office Street incorporated important Roman walling and was well worthy of careful preservation and retention.

The Southernhay Car Park gave easy access to the new shopping centre.

The Age of the Car – and Car Parks

A significant factor in replanning the city centre was ensuring adequate car parking space. The loss of buildings at the top of Southernhay West helped provide a large open space that was ideal. Backing on to the City Wall, better access was given after the removal of an archway in the wall at the rear of St John's School. An electricity substation was located in the City Wall, near Bedford Street, later removed. More car parking space became available in Paris Street with the building of the bus station.

A new-style pay kiosk with barriers was erected at the Southernhay West Car Park. The side wall of the electricity substation is shown left.

Southernhay West Car Park is shown completed and surrounded by flower beds defined by Heavitree stone. The eastern angle tower on the City Wall was restored and the stretch of wall in the new Post Office Street retained and tidied up. This featured a particularly good stretch of original Roman stone work.

The concept of stone walling for flower beds was to be used in other parts of the city. In Catherine Street new underground toilets had been constructed to replace the pre-war ones in Bedford Street. The entrances to these facilities were to be obscured by the use of raised beds planted with flowers and shrubs, helping to give the street a more pleasant look, particularly in the summer months. Flower beds were also constructed against St Stephen's Church.

View across Southernhay to the car park and Cathedral. The City Wall is shown after the removal of the archway that led from St John's School. The spire of St Mary Major Church stands behind, adjacent to the newly built corner of Catherine Street.

Rebuilding of High Street

One of Exeter's most well-known landmarks, the corner of Bedford Street and High Street, was cleared of the remains of Lloyds Bank and the famous Dellers Café. The removal proved more difficult than at first assumed, owing to the substantial construction of the buildings. The bank was to take up temporary premises at Rowe Bros & Co, opposite Central Station. The move was advertised by a large sign board displayed at the top of the corner steps that had led into the bank, shown bottom centre.

Lloyds Bank in temporary premises at Rowe Bros, Queen Street.

For a period of time it was usual to see the remaining ground-floor foundations of cleared buildings in the High Street. The classical façade of the Commercial Union Assurance Company building had remained standing, but was demolished. The new building was to bear no resemblance to its former appearance. In order to continue business the company moved to the Rougemont Hotel in Queen Street, with its administrative branch at Altamira at Topsham.

The Commercial Union Assurance Company Limited operated from the ground floor of the Rougemont Hotel during the early-postwar years. The windows of the hotel bore the company name in gilded lettering, stating also Fire–Life–Accident–Marine–Engineering –Livestock.

Much of High Street was to be used for temporary car parking prior to rebuilding. The view shown looks across High Street to a building that was originally a nineteenth-century chapel. In 1947 it is listed as Castle Street Hall & Sunday School and also the Royal Navy and Army Recruiting Centre. A recruiting notice is shown on its frontage and also on an exterior wall. A new road was created in front of the building and named Bailey Street. Unfortunately, the work resulted in the collapse of the retaining wall of the chapel that is seen shorn up in this record. The building to the right is the rebuilt end property of Northernhay Place.

Exeter High Street is shown in its original width just before the London Inn Square and Paris Street. Temporary shops are shown at Eastgate and part of the original City Wall still stands opposite, but was later removed.

READERS' LETTERS

The New Exeter

Sir,—Reflecting on the many interesting and controversial letters which have appeared in your paper from time to time, two striking facts are outstanding.

Firstly, the apparent lack of interest in the new Exeter planning shown by women, and secondly, no correspondent has suggested the need for deep underground shelters. Although not a pessimist, the writer does not believe in wishful thinking to the extent of eliminating future and possibly more terrible wars than this one. Only deep shelters can offer complete protection against modern weapons, and we owe it to the future generation that we are not accused of lack of foresight.

It is better to be safe than sorry!

"F.," Exeter, 1-1-45.

Exeter High Street was for a period of time a wide-open space uncharacteristically devoid of buildings as seen here at the junction with Castle Street in June 1950.

The foundations for a new Marks & Spencer store are recorded on 1 August 1950. To the right are shown Castle Street and the remaining single storey of the National Westminster Bank. The whole of the central area was, at this time, laid bare of buildings and being used for random car parking, allowing an uninterrupted view to the Cathedral.

The enclosed site for the new Marks & Spencer allowed public viewing from Castle Street. Works were carried out by Bovis. A temporary street sign for Castle Street is shown in High Street, bottom right.

In December 1950 the construction of Marks & Spencer's High Street store was well under way. Large cranes had been brought on site to lift steel girders into position. The citizens of Exeter would become familiar with such scenes as the city continued to be rebuilt over a period of nearly thirty years.

Exeter High Street in July 1951 showing Marks & Spencer well on the way to completion.

Barclays Bank on the corner of High Street and Bedford Street was severely damaged during the raid of 4 May 1942. The ground floor of the building survived and in order to continue business the first floor was reconstructed. The building was the last to be demolished in the High Street, clearing away the last link with the street's pre-war image. The entry to Bedford Circus is shown right, and still has its original lamppost.

READERS LETTERS

"Women Are Interested In Exeter II."

Sir,—I would like to protest against women being accused of lack of interest in Exeter II. Surely some have offered their help on the Housing Committee; my own letter was published as early as July 15th, 1942.

I also remember reading a suggestion about a large car park under Northernhay which would provide, in any future war, air raid accommodation. The idea was originally, I think, from a Birmingham reader, who may have been staying here. He mentioned the many entrances that could be provided in such a car park, and what a revenue it would be to the city! Is anyone keeping a scrapbook of these good ideas? Here is one other: that we hold the municipal election in the summer instead of the depth of winter.

EVA STORRY.
90, Cowick-lane, Exeter.

In 1948 building licences instigating the first stages of reconstruction became available. The first section to get under way in High Street was opposite the junction with Bedford Street, with the building of Pearl Assurance House and a number of new shop units. It is shown from the site used for the construction of the service road for Princesshay. The south side of the street was still used for parking.

Bedford Street to High Street is shown with Barclays Bank and its rebuilt first floor. The street still retains the central railed underground toilets, and the new road has yet to be built.

The north side of High Street was the site for Pearl Assurance House and the Commercial Union building, with offices on the upper floors. New retailers taking up ground-floor shops included Thos Cook & Son, Kendall, umbrella makers, costumiers Harolds, and three shoe retailers, Phillips, Woodleys and Dolcis Dolores.

The new road has been laid out in Bedford Street. Lloyds Bank has yet to be completed and Martins Bank, at the corner of Catherine Street, is under construction, left. No building had been finished on the east side of Bedford Street which later was to include the end of Princesshay and the Post Office. Photo c.1953.

The junction of Bedford Street with High Street is shown with Pearl Assurance House and Commercial Union buildings. The old Barclays Bank on the corner of the street, right, has been painted and new central traffic bollards positioned in High Street to assist with directing the two-way traffic. A Wall's ice-cream van had parked next to one of the new-style lampposts.

The Commercial Union premises brought a more austere style to the High Street. Heavy metal double doors bear the company's logo, a figure of Alfred the Great and the wording 'West of England Fire and Life Assurance Company'. Above the doors is a crest consisting of two winged lions with the wording Anchora Salutis. *Decorative wrought-iron work was added to the arched windows.*

Lloyds Bank took the longest to complete of all the High Street buildings owing to the security requirements for its vaults. The early stages of construction are shown, dwarfing W H Smith & Son who were operating from a small stall in High Street.

W H Smith & Son opened new premises at No. 233 High Street, adjacent to Lloyds Bank. Offices above are being advertised by Leslie Fulford operating from 5 Goldsmith Street and Husseys, 17 Gandy Street. The British General Insurance Company and the Ocean Accident & Guarantee Corporation were already in residence. The latter had, pre-war, operated from the corner of South Street and High Street.

High Street is shown before the completion of Lloyds Bank which is still shrouded in scaffolding.

The completed Lloyds Bank in High Street.

Interior of Lloyds Bank, High Street.

The corner of Castle Street and High Street was widened considerably to allow better vehicle access to the Courts and Exeter Castle. This record of the Westminster Bank clearly shows the extent to which High Street had been pushed back from its original width. At the end of the street the blank side wall of No. 229 High Street faced the pedestrian. Beyond are older buildings which had survived the blitz of May 1942.

The Westminster Bank incorporated two shops units, taken by shoe chain Lennards and McGahey the Tobacconist. Behind the bank was the Telephone Exchange, leading up to the Castle. It narrowly escaped destruction in the raid of May 1942 and was only saved by the efforts of its dedicated staff.

The new design for central Exeter received considerable criticism for having a monolithic style throughout the whole length of High Street, well illustrated by the nearly completed north side of High Street seen in 1955. However, shops were spacious and display windows larger. Two-way traffic continued for a period of time and pavements had been made far wider

The well-known pre-war company of Mark Rowe furnishers had previously occupied a building on the same site. Its premises had been partly built from the stones of the demolished East Gate and had displayed a statue of Henry VII. Removal of the gate in 1784 had been marked by a bronze plaque attached to the right side of the window frame. The replacement post-war building was opened in 1954.

The architectural style adopted for High Street allowed for little individuality between the shops units. The top south side of High Street had been the site of the East Gate Arcade, the National Provincial Bank and the General Post Office. The new block led into Princesshay, with six shops facing the High Street, which at this point were Wolfe & Hollander, True-Form, Hope Brothers, Lipton and Paige.

The development of High Street continued from the top south side, towards Bedford Street. The design incorporated an arcade giving access into the new Princesshay, built on the site of St John's School and its playground. Pre-war an entry existed from High Street that gave direct access into St John's School. Taken in 1955 this photograph records five shop units that are to be completed but Timothy Whites Household Stores are about to open, seen right, and Daniel Neal has opened near the Arcade.

The west-corner site of High Street with Bedford Street was rebuilt creating six shops units and offices. Retailers operating from these premises in the mid-1960s were Lewis, separates, Alexandre, tailors, Faiman, gowns, Manfield, shoes, and on the Bedford Street side the National Fur Company and Mitchell, jeweller. The newly built Martins Bank is shown on the corner of Catherine Street at the rear of the building.

In October 1953 the new building on the site of Dellers Café was being completed on the Catherine Street side. It was to become Stephen House, taking its name from the adjacent church, with an entrance from Catherine Street.

An aerial view of c.*1955 gives a clear indication of the extent of redevelopment in the central area of Exeter. The High Street is shown nearly completed, except for Barclays Bank on the corner of Bedford Street and Boots on the corner of the London Inn Square. East Gate was yet to be rebuilt and Princesshay to be completed on the north side. Over fifty per cent of Bedford Street had been constructed but the Post Office was yet to be begun.*

A view from the south, towards High Street. The City Wall is shown in the foreground. The south side of Princesshay and the Post Office have yet to be built.

By 1979, Exeter High Street had been banned to cars, with buses only allowed, and had been narrowed by fifty per cent in its upper part leading to Sidwell Street. Trees, together with flower beds and seating, became a decorative feature to detract from the blandness of the street. Its unimaginative character and dearth of interest still caused plenty of comment, however.

High Street 1955.

Marks & Spencer

The new Marks & Spencer store is shown with its Castle Street entrance, left. No other buildings had been erected on this part of the High Street at this time.

Marks & Spencer was one of the most prominent new stores in Exeter High Street, taking up new premises on 10 November 1951. The company had been bombed out of their original premises, Nos 174 to 178 Fore Street, and there had been a number of fatalities. The new site, incorporating the corner of Castle Street, boasted a wider thoroughfare than pre-war.

The spacious windows of Marks & Spencer allowed greater opportunities for tempting window displays to entice customers through the two sets of double doors that opened on to High Street.

A new feature at the Marks & Spencer store was a large Café Bar with counter seating. The Café Bar menu offers: 'Baked beans on toast 6d., tea & coffee 2d., ice-cream 2d. & 4d., cooled crush 2d., Horlicks with milk 5d., egg rolls 4d., fish, chips & peas 10d. No orders taken after 5.45pm.'

An array of summer dresses on sale at 35s.11d.

The latest thing… Marks & Spencer Marspun dresses are a snip at 32s.11d.

Smarter daywear is on offer too…

Socks galore, and this is only the children's section…

Behind the scenes, sample lines have to be checked and selected.

It's crunch time for all biscuit-lovers. Will it be the Campbell's Lincoln at 9d., the strawberry creams, 9d., or the fruit shortcake at 1s?

Pre-email and memo, staff are kept up to speed with all the latest, posted on the company's St Michael's News *Exeter Edition bulletin board.*

As staff add up the day's takings, a poster behind them still seems to echo wartime austerity, stating 'If you don't need it don't buy it!'

Boots the Chemists

Left: *Boots the Chemists began construction of new premises in 1956 on the corner of the London Inn Square and the site of the destroyed Plaza Cinema. Opposite can be seen the temporary shops at Eastgate, adjacent to the Exeter Cooperative Society Ltd. Pre-war, Boots had been located at 223 & 224 High Street on the corner of Queen Street.*

Below: *The building of Boots the Chemists, as viewed from High Street. The corner of Northernhay Place is seen right.*

The store's design included a railed balcony overlooking High Street and a wide round-cornered concrete canopy designed to give added protection to customers. Photo 1957.

Disaster struck on Saturday 5 October 1957 when the newly erected canopy collapsed on the High Street side, narrowly missing customers. The whole front section had to be removed and rebuilt.

Top brass were on hand for the official opening of the store's new High Street premises on 31 October 1957.

A month later the huge first floor with its new-style interior was decorated and piled high with cards and gift items, ready for Christmas 1957.

Customers flock into the new High Street store, November 1957.

A New Era in Shopping

Colsons' models of 1948 display the latest thing in style.

Colsons celebrate their long history in go-ahead style with a Hat Cavalcade of 'stylish hats for over 100 years' in their High Street display windows. Photo c.1952.

All the ingredients for a comfortable home on display in Colsons' furniture department.

The latest in 'contemporay style' from Wrightons, on display in Colsons' furniture department: a two-drawer chest of drawers for £14.19s.6d., a wing-back chair for £26.6s.0d., a Continental bedstead at £11.5s.6d., and a bedroom dresser at £33.17s.6d.

Colsons' 'Fabrics into Fashions' promotion of April 1949 was part of the launch of the store's new premises, and showed off their range of fabrics available to home dressmakers, still very much a way of life for many women.

A number of well-known shops could be found in High Street, near the junction with South Street, in the early-postwar years. They included The House of Moons, who sold pianos, records, radios and televisions, and F W Woolworth & Co. Ltd, next door in large premises with double-fronted display windows. Today it is occupied by McDonald's.

Moons was advertised as 'The Centre of Music in Exeter' and supplied all the latest hits! Customers wishing to 'try before you buy' could use the listening booths, seen to the left of the counter.

Home entertainment of the late 1950s/early 1960s, with everything from pianos and radios to the new-fangled Hi-Fis and televisions, on show at Moons.

Trumpeter Eddy Calvert signs autographs for delighted fans at Moons in High Street on a guest visit of 16 April 1955.

Postwar redevelopment at the top of Fore Street allowed it to be widened near its junction with South Street and North Street, with new buildings being constructed further back from the road than pre-war. British Home Stores acquired a site previously occupied by Marks & Spencer, a dairy and Gospel Hall. The move was considered temporary but they are still trading from the same premises after nearly fifty years. Photo 1954.

The site opposite British Home Stores was also designated for new shops. The road adjacent to the old Lower Market was previously Milk Street, leading to a small square containing an obelisk marking the spot of a water conduit. It survived the blitz of 1942 but was demolished to allow development to continue.

The loss of buildings at the top of Fore Street created opportunities for new development on the site of the pre-war Milk Street which ran down the side of the Lower Market, from Fore Street to Guinea Street. New shops on the site were Weaver to Wearer and Henry Turner, furnishers. The photo shows the original road surface from Milk Street still intact but the street and its name were later lost.

Upper Fore Street, on the south side, is shown nearly complete but work is still in progress on St George's Hall. A new block was built next to Weaver to Wearer and was to be the new Chevalier Inn. The building, however, in no way compared with its historical pre-war predecessor. Photo 1961.

The north side of upper Fore Street was rebuilt from British Home Stores to the corner of Mary Arches Street. The entry into the old pre-war Mary Arches Street had been narrow but was considerably widened and the corner building rounded. New occupants included Pooles, pianos, carpets, radio and television, Vane Socks & Stockings and shoe retailers Olivers. Photo May 1955.

WATTYS DELICATESSEN

13 MARTINS LANE, EXETER · *Telephone 56654*

(A few yards from Cathedral Close and Royal Clarence Hotel)

CONTINENTAL & ORIENTAL FOODS
FROM 50 COUNTRIES

CHOICE OF CHEESES FROM 80 VARIETIES

SALAMI, COOKED MEATS, PIES, CANNED AND FROZEN FOODS, ROAST CHICKEN, UNCOOKED CHICKEN, TURKEY, SMOKED SALMON, TROUT, EEL, OYSTERS, CAVIAR

TOP QUALITY GROCERIES

CREAM BY POST **FRESHLY GROUND COFFEE**

PARCELS AND HAMPERS SENT TO ANY PART OF THE WORLD

'*A Private Enterprise*'

Proprietor—E. S. ASTON

Management and staff at the newly opened Vane Socks & Stockings, Fore Street. Photo May 1955.

Lipton the Grocers opened opposite Marks & Spencer on the south side of High Street. A familiar face on every British high street, its front window exhorted customers 'This way to Lipton for quality, value and civility'.

Old-fashioned service and style was the order of the day at Lipton's No. 6 High Street premises, May 1952.

Manfield's shoe shop in High Street creates a new style and displays an intriguing innovation – a machine capable of visually assessing the feet of clients to ensure a proper fit!

On completion of Princesshay McGahey the Tobacconist acquired a small kiosk at Eastgate House at the top of Princesshay. Above were the offices of the Inland Revenue, Factory Inspector, Ministry of Labour, Official Receiver, Board of Trade and Ministry of Works.

In 1953 Wymans' book shop in High Street created an eyecatching coronation window advertising the forthcoming 'Souvenir Book of the Year', Elizabeth Our Queen *by Richard Dimbleby, price 'only' 12s.6d. 'The book everybody is talking about', containing eight full-colour portraits and 32 pages of pictures, was on sale from 30 March.*

South Street Reconstruction

South Street was devastated in May 1942 by the effects of heavy bombing and fires from incendiaries. The east side, a row of stuccoed buildings, collapsed like a pack of cards and The Hall of the Vicars Choral, seen through one of the remaining archways of the Lower Market, was left in ruins. The Cathedral's Great West Window was blown out and is shown covered.

The derelict area on the west side of South Street was to be used for casual parking. Remarkably, the church of St Mary Major, standing in the Cathedral Yard, escaped destruction. The property of W V Cole & Son Printers, the College Works, is shown in Kalendarhay, beside the ruin of Hall of the Vicars Choral. The company had outlets at Nos 87 & 88 South Street. T Willey and Dalley Sanitary & Electrical Engineers advertise on the side of 1 Cathedral Yard, one of the remaining medieval buildings called 'Three Gables', adjacent to the church.

Fore Street is shown at the junction with South Street, after the clearance of blitz rubble. The obelisk shown far left marked the site of an ancient conduit and stood in the small courtyard off Milk Street, left. It was later demolished.

In 1954 South Street was widened by over 50 per cent and the new road surface laid by hand. Temporary stalls were erected by retailers who had lost their premises on the east side of the street.

Purpose-built, temporary wooden huts were provided in lower South Street, adjacent to Bear Lane, for use by retailers.

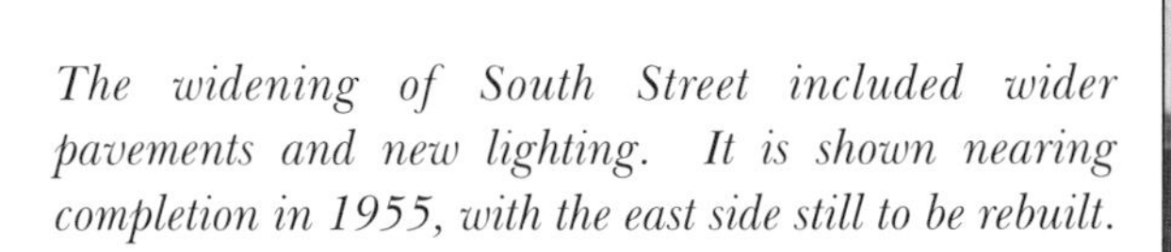

The widening of South Street included wider pavements and new lighting. It is shown nearing completion in 1955, with the east side still to be rebuilt.

The corner junction site of South Street with High Street was destroyed by incendiary bombs in May 1942. The buildings of D Forte & Sons, dining rooms, Milk Bar and Fried Fish Dealers, Palmer & Edwards, bakers, and Cyril Patch Pork Butcher were gutted. The Globe Hotel, at the rear of the buildings, was also destroyed. Properties backing on to the cleared site were covered by tarpaulins until rebuilding started. A new entry into Cathedral Yard was created in 1960.

An aerial view of c.1956 shows the west side of South Street virtually complete though work was yet to start on the east side.

At the corner of South Street and High Street, shown around 1961, the new pedestrian access into Cathedral Yard has a false wall to block off the rear of older buildings. The ruin of the Hall of the Vicars Choral was retained and left as a memorial (seen right) to the victims of the Exeter Blitz in May 1942.

The corner site of South Street with Coombe Street was used for the new £300 000 building for Commercial Union Assurance Group, named Concorde House and opened in 1962. It was designed to house the city's first computer named 'Cutie', its technical name being Commercial Union Totally Integrated Electronics. Cutie was actually so large she had to be hoisted by crane into the building, remaining there for five years.

Paris Street - Bus Station and the Civic Centre

Pre-war Paris Street led from Sidwell Street to Heavitree Road, where it joined with Russell Street at the Triangle in Newtown. The narrow street was lined with older properties, some of which survived wartime damage, including the Elim Chapel, shown here. The area between Paris Street and Summerland Street contained a high density of dwellings, some with access through covered passages, alleyways and courtyards. This area was cleared of all remaining buildings during 1959 and 1960 and the road pattern changed.

The new corner of Paris Street is shown, looking up Sidwell Street. The whole of Paris Street was cleared and later all remaining properties in Sidwell Street were pulled down, which with future redevelopment resulted in a characterless street.

Lower Paris Street was used as a temporary car park before the building of the bus and coach station.

The area between Paris Street and a new Verney Street became the new bus and coach station, with an upper and lower concourse. The facilities also included a car park at the rear of new buildings in Paris Street. Photo c. *1967.*

The bus station newly completed in 1965.

The new bus station, replacing its predecessor in Paul Street, included a sloping concrete canopy to protect waiting passengers from the elements. New shops, a restaurant and public information facility were integrated into the design. Photo c.1964.

With the redevelopment of Paris Street, Dix's Field, was chosen as the location for a new Civic Centre at a cost of £1 million. Originally a more extensive development was planned but it was ultimately reduced to three buildings: Phase One, Phase Two and the Banking Hall. The construction of the Centre involved the removal of existing period buildings in Dix's Field on the east side. Only the south-west corner survived.

The period houses, dating from 1805, were designed by Matthew Nosworthy, an Exeter architect. The interiors still contained some interesting features including corbels, cast-iron balustrade and fanlights, a pillared door and circular-headed window. The City Architect stated that the items would be retained and that 'the corbels may be put into the new civic buildings'. Demolition started in 1969 to make way for the new Civic Centre. A report later stated: 'The terrace was classified as a building of architectural merit and it was unquestionably important to preserve the external façades as they were an essential part of the pre-war city.'

The two new buildings would be 58ft high and constructed from precast units. City Architect Mr Vinton Hall, responsible for their design, stated: 'It is my intention to develop the façades with a strongly modelled pre-cast fenestrational element, finished in Bath or Portland Stone.' He added: 'I am quite convinced Exeter has more than its sufficiency of red-and-buff brick buildings, which if used to excess give a raw and rather coarse tonal quality to newly developed areas.'

The foundation stone for the Civic Centre was laid in April 1969 by Mayor of Exeter, Alderman J B Martin. It brought all elements of the authority under one roof and replaced the outdated offices in Southernhay West. The initial concept was to lay the complex out in campus style and would, it was thought, make it easier for the public to locate the various departments. The scheme, however, was never completed, owing to a lack of funds.

Various Buildings

The destruction of Paris Street and its adjacent areas in 1942 led to the extensive clearance of remaining buildings, courtyards, alleyways and almshouses. Hurste's Almshouses stood in Belgrave Road, just off old Paris Street, and consisted of a row of early-nineteenth-century houses endowed by William Hurste, Mayor of Exeter. These were demolished to allow the continuation of development in Paris Street and the building of the bus station. The site of the houses, removed in 1959, is now where the bus station lower concourse overlooks the Paris Street roundabout.

Hurste's Almshouses showing the original half doors, bracketed gas lamp and foundation stone bearing the wording 'Built and Endowed AD MDL XVIII by W Hurste Esq. who was five times Mayor of this City. Rebuilt 1819 T. Floud Esq. Mayor'.

St Edmund's Church narrowly escaped total destruction with the building of Western Way inner bypass. The church, substantially rebuilt in the mid-nineteenth century, maintained the tradition of chapels connected to the medieval Exe Bridge. Though mostly demolished, a late decision saved its tower and the remaining body of the church. The building could have served a useful purpose as an historical Interpretation Centre for the West Quarter and Riverside. It is shown without its roof but with all walls standing.

Follett Buildings, a four-storey brick tenement block, situated on the north side of Coombe Street, was built to rehouse the city's poorer families who were from the West Quarter. The building offered an extensive view over Exeter Quay and the surrounding area.

Built in 1874 by a company called the Improved Industrial Dwellings Company, and named after the Chief Magistrate, Follett Buildings, had an imposing and austere look.

The site of Follett Buildings included Mermaids Yard, taking its name from an ancient inn that had existed on the site. A small square was formed by the building of further houses in the late-twentieth century, known as Cottons Buildings. The whole site was demolished in the late 1970s.

The demolition of Mermaids Yard, along with Cottons Buildings and Follett Buildings in 1979.

Exeter's riverside areas were subject to profound change during the 1960s and 70s with the construction of new bridges and the Flood Prevention Scheme. The City Brewery, that stood just off Exe Bridge on Commercial Road, was removed, together with the prominent building used by Gilchrist & Fisher for manufacturing leather-goods. Photo 1957.

Situated off Black Aller Weir, Head Weir Mill was used for the production of paper. By 1978 the extensive building was empty and in a ruinous state. Within a short period of time parts of the property were demolished. The remaining original building was converted into a riverside pub, the Mill on the Exe.

The Floods

The River Exe has played a vital role in the development of Exeter but its close proximity to dwellings on the west side of the city has always been a problem. Flooding has been a regular occurrence throughout the centuries and the lower reaches of the Exe still flood each winter as millions of gallons of water head seawards. The flooding of the 1960s proved exceptional. The River Exe is shown at the 1905 Exe Bridge, as the water level rises. The foreground shows the river's edge at the old Cattle Market in Bonhay Road. Photo 1968, 1.55pm.

The River Exe is shown with the water level rising and overflowing into Okehampton Street. No. 1 Exe Bridge is shown, left, and opposite is the City Brewery in Commercial Road. At No. 73 in the same road, centre, is Gilchrist & Fisher, leather goods manufacturers, who occupied a substantial waterside property.

In 1962 rising water from the river created problems for vehicles in Okehampton Street. At this time a new roundabout had been created at the junction with Alphington Street, Cowick Street and Okehampton Street.

On 3 December 1960 a heavy downpour turned the River Exe into a raging torrent that surged into St Thomas, causing chaos and damage to property. The river is shown sweeping over the banks, creating a huge swirling channel in Okehampton Street and reaching up to 6ft deep.

Another record of 3 December 1960, showing St Thomas is flooded and Okehampton Street cut off.

Water levels build up in Alphington Street as the River Exe bursts its banks in December 1960.

Roads off Alphington Street become lakes as the River Exe engulfs the St Thomas area, again in the 1960s. Sydney Road is awash but the local post office is still open for business.

Residents in the Sydney Road area of St Thomas show true Dunkirk spirit as they stand up to their ankles in flood water at the post office.

It's all an adventure for these children and a dog at Exwick in 1960.

Moving through the flood water proves a challenge for a vehicle in Exwick.

Escape for some from the engulfed Royal Oak pub in Okehampton Street, but no walkies in prospect for the dog left behind.

The Exe Valley under water in 1960.

The Inner Bypass

The construction of the Inner Bypass to the south of the city was started in 1954, from Belmont Road to Summerland Street. The project, staged in three phases, was to be responsible for demolition on an unprecedented scale. In particular, the final phase completed in the mid-1960s decimated the western side of Exeter. The buildings shown at the junction with Blackboy Road were removed in the first phase of the project. To the immediate right is the entry into Belmont Road c.1954.

The junction of Sidwell Street with Belmont Road was marked by railed underground toilets and the fountain dedicated to surgeon Arthur Kempe. The fountain was retained and removed to a new site adjacent to St Anne's Almshouses, and new underground toilets built c.1954.

All of the buildings in this view at the top of Belmont Road, near its junction with Sidwell Street, were demolished. When constructed, the Inner Bypass woul link up with a new roundabout to be created at the bottom of Paris Street.

This aerial view of c.1955 clearly shows the course of the new Inner Bypass. It is intersected by Denmark Road and Barnfield Road as it heads towards Magdalen Bridge. The section from Denmark Road, was created by filling in a natural valley of orchards with hundreds of tons of wartime rubble from destroyed city buildings. At the junction with Magdalen Street the whole area was demolished, including some interesting and important historic buildings.

From 1961, during Phase Three of the project, from Holloway Street to the river was systematically removed, which not only included buildings in the direct path of the new road but properties well away from the Inner Bypass. The view looks from the intersection with Coombe Street to Holloway Street.

At the junction with Coombe Street a pedestrian underpass was created, effectively truncating the street. The concrete sides of the underpass are shown under construction.

To obtain the correct approach to the riverside the lower section of Western Way was banked as it approached Edmund Street, resulting in the cutting off of West Street. Traditionally the street had continued from St Mary Steps Church directly across the top of the City Wall to the Quay. Cricklepit Mill is shown right, with the small dwellings known as Leat Terrace, later also demolished.

To complete the gyratory road scheme leading to and from the proposed new Exe Bridges, Frog Street had to be demolished. It would eventually become the route for incoming traffic from Exe Bridge South. Vehicles would pass through Exe Island and under new Bridge Street.

Shilhay - End of Exeter's Industrial Area

READERS' LETTERS

'OUR WASTED RIVERSIDE'

Sir,—"City Talk," by "Cit," of your issue, November 25th, which contained a Yorkshireman's opinion of our wasted riverside, interested me. I share his views.

Surely something could be done to hide those tumbledown buildings and to brighten the hideous piece of waste ground. I include the useless, out-of-date children's playground which is used for the sole purpose of a fairground on Bank Holidays. A good example is the way in which the town of Bedford has laid out lawns and gardens, complete with bandstand on the banks of the River Ouse, turning what would be an ugly stretch of water into a lovely promenade, where, on a Sunday afternoon, one can see what seems to be the whole population enjoying its after-lunch walk.

Come on, Exeter! or "Ee by gum, lad, the generation that comes back from the war will see to it that Exeter gets a move on."

EXONIAN.

India.

Exeter's traditional industrial area, Shilhay, is shown around 1960 as a compact area of industrial buildings. Created by land drainage over the centuries the area was divided by a leat known as Coney Lake, used for offloading on to industrial sites. In medieval times Shilhay was an area used for the drying of woollen cloth; timber yards, tanneries, foundries, candle factories, skin and bone merchants, corn mills and other activities were also concentrated there. Here, West Street still exists without alteration, with Tremletts Tannery, shown centre bottom, and opposite, St Edmund's Church. Commercial Road ran from Exe Bridge to the Quay. Haven Banks, opposite Shilhay, was the favourite site for travelling fairs. Within a short period of time the whole of this area was removed for redevelopment and the construction of the Exeter Flood Prevention Scheme around 1960.

The higher and lower leats flowed through Shilhay beside the City Wall and along the edge of Commercial Road. The lower leat was mostly culverted after the redevelopment of Shilhay. On the higher leat stood Cricklepit Mill, which had been used as a corn mill by W G Shears. Remaining within the building was the original water-wheel and on the higher leat outside, there was a second wheel. Further down the leat were sluice gates and another water-wheel originally part of Lower Mills. Unfortunately, this wheel and its gates were removed. Photo February 1970.

A view from Colleton Cresent shows the River Exe and the edge of Shilhay in 1964. On the river bank can be seen the timber-drying sheds of Gabriel, Wade & English, importers of timber and ten test fibre board. Nearby was Pearse & Co Marine Store, dealers in rag, rope, metal, rabbit skins, horsehair, old iron and waste paper buyers. Photo 1964.

A view from the City Wall shows the joining of the higher and lower leats at Quay Bridge, leading out into the River Exe. The small brick-arched bridge on the right is shown over the higher leat and would have given access to the original Lower Mills. The industrial properties on the edge of the leats were garages, workshops and electrical engineers. Photo February 1970.

In the late 1960s Shilhay was cleared of all buildings except one, Shilhay House, which was left standing and became a Refuge Centre for the homeless. The redevelopment of the area and how it should be used became a contentious issue. While one body of opinion favoured the area being used for leisure purposes and the possible creation of major sports facilities, the area was finally designated for housing. Photo January 1970.

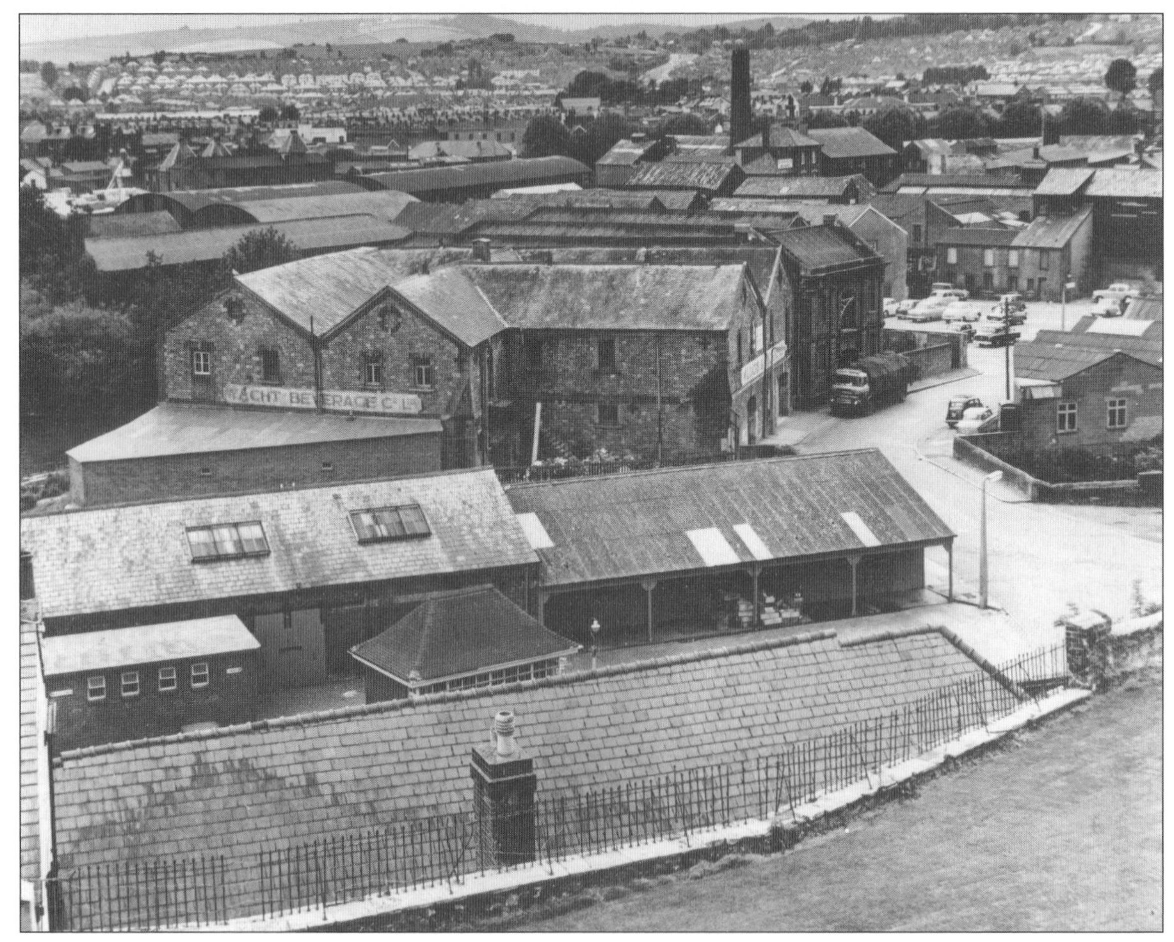

A view of 1970 overlooks the Quay from Friars Hill. Directly below is the roof of the DIY store building which, after some historical investigations, was recognised as being the original Quay transit shed, dating from 1680. It was restored by the City Council in 1987 as part of the redevelopment of the Quay and area. The small structure in front of the building was the public weighing scales, and to the left were the public conveniences, both later demolished. The early-nineteenth-century transit shed beyond is shown with its later asbestos roof extension, which was also removed, bringing the shed back to its original size. Fish was stored on ice in this building. The large bonded warehouses belonging to the Kennaway family, seen beyond, became Exeter's first night-club, the Quay Club. It provided young Exeter people with the first real venue of its type in the city and established a reputation for dancing. Photo January 1970.

The creation of Exeter's Flood Prevention Scheme was to have a huge impact on the riverside and nearby properties. Steel piles were driven along the whole of river bank from Exwick to Trews Weir, and the banks reinforced with concrete, as here at Shilhay. The church of St Edmund is still intact in Edmund Street.

This record, taken in January 1970, looks up to Exe Bridge from Haven Banks. Most buildings on Shilhay have been removed and a concrete riverside walkway has been created. The old Exe Bridge remains, but adjacent to it in Commercial Road the City Brewery is being demolished.

Exe Island and Frog Street

Exe Island was created over centuries by the drainage of marshland and became an industrial area based around the city's leats. In the nineteenth and twentieth centuries foundries, gasworks, abattoirs and the livestock market were based there. In the eighteenth century the area was partly enclosed by the construction of a viaduct leading to the Exe Bridge. It became New Bridge Street. The structure featured a fine arched entrance that connected directly with Exe Island. Underneath the arch was the date 1772. Latterly a painted notice-board simply stated 'entrance to Exe Island'. Photo 1961.

The construction of Western Way sounded the death knell for the Exe Island archway, the passing of another familiar feature of the city. To allow the new Inner Bypass to reach the river it was scheduled for removal and initially a new bridge was partly built and the archway demolished in sections, as shown in this record. To the right, and seen below the road, is the original Victorian Exe Island School for Boys & Girls which had a small playground to one side. This too was demolished to allow the new road to continue to the river. Photo 1961.

Along with the Exe Island entrance, an early slate-covered five-storeyed building was also removed from Exe Island to give greater width to the new road. Buildings in New Bridge Street on the opposite road suffered the same fate.

In Exe Island, and adjacent to the Queen Victoria Public House, stood the Exe Island & City Mission's buildings. Entry to the Hall was by a covered passage-way seen bottom right and signed The Full Gospel. An entrance also existed from New Bridge Street via an aerial tunnel. Removal of the Mission terrace robbed this intimate square of much of its character. Photo 1961.

Another large chunk of the eighteenth-century archway is consigned to the bulldozer. Photo 1961.

The completed single-section concrete bridge, with the remains of the original eighteenth-century viaduct, yet to be removed.

The completed Inner Bypass and concrete bridge at New Bridge Street. Construction of the road obliterated much of West Street, removing Ewings Lane, Frog Street, much of New Bridge Street and Exe Island. Photo 1962.

A number of workers' dwellings survived until the mid-1960s. St Edmund's Square at the end of Tudor Street provided houses for local workers.

'The House That Moved'

No. 16 Edmund Street stood at the corner of Edmund Street and Frog Street and was to become one of the most famous buildings in the South West of England. The ancient origins of the tiny timber-framed dwelling had been well documented by historians and in the 1930s some restoration work was done. Despite this the building fell into such a sad state of disrepair, as shown in this record of 1960, that suggestions were mooted in the 1950s that it should be demolished.

A Preservation Order by the Ministry of Works saved No. 16 – dating from around 1430 and certainly unique in the South West – from the prospect of obliteration. It was to be nearly ten years, however, before the final solution was agreed – to physically move the house. In 1961 the framework was shored up with timber and the building lifted off its ancient site, where it had stood for nearly 600 years.

The method devised for the operation involved fitting it with wheels and winching it to a new site just 100 yards away. The move was carefully planned, with the first stage being to rest in Edmund Street.

Iron rails were laid on the street into which the wheels were carefully guided. By means of a winch located in West Street the house was gradually pulled upwards to its new site on the corner of Edmund Street.

As the house approached the Teignmouth Inn at the corner of Ewings Lane, the structure jammed on the edge of the kerb. The problem was soon overcome by the use of a saw and the move continued. The Teignmouth Inn, a mock timber-framed building, was demolished, together with its neighbours, after the moving of the house.

Exeter personality Freddie Collins recorded the moving of No. 16 Edmund Street. Freddie was for thirty years a photographer for the Plymouth-based Western Morning News, *and retired in 1984. He was often seen working around Exeter and was known for his charismatic personality.*

The moving of Exeter's oldest dwelling created worldwide news and put the city briefly on the tourist map as reporters and onlookers descended to capture this rare moment.

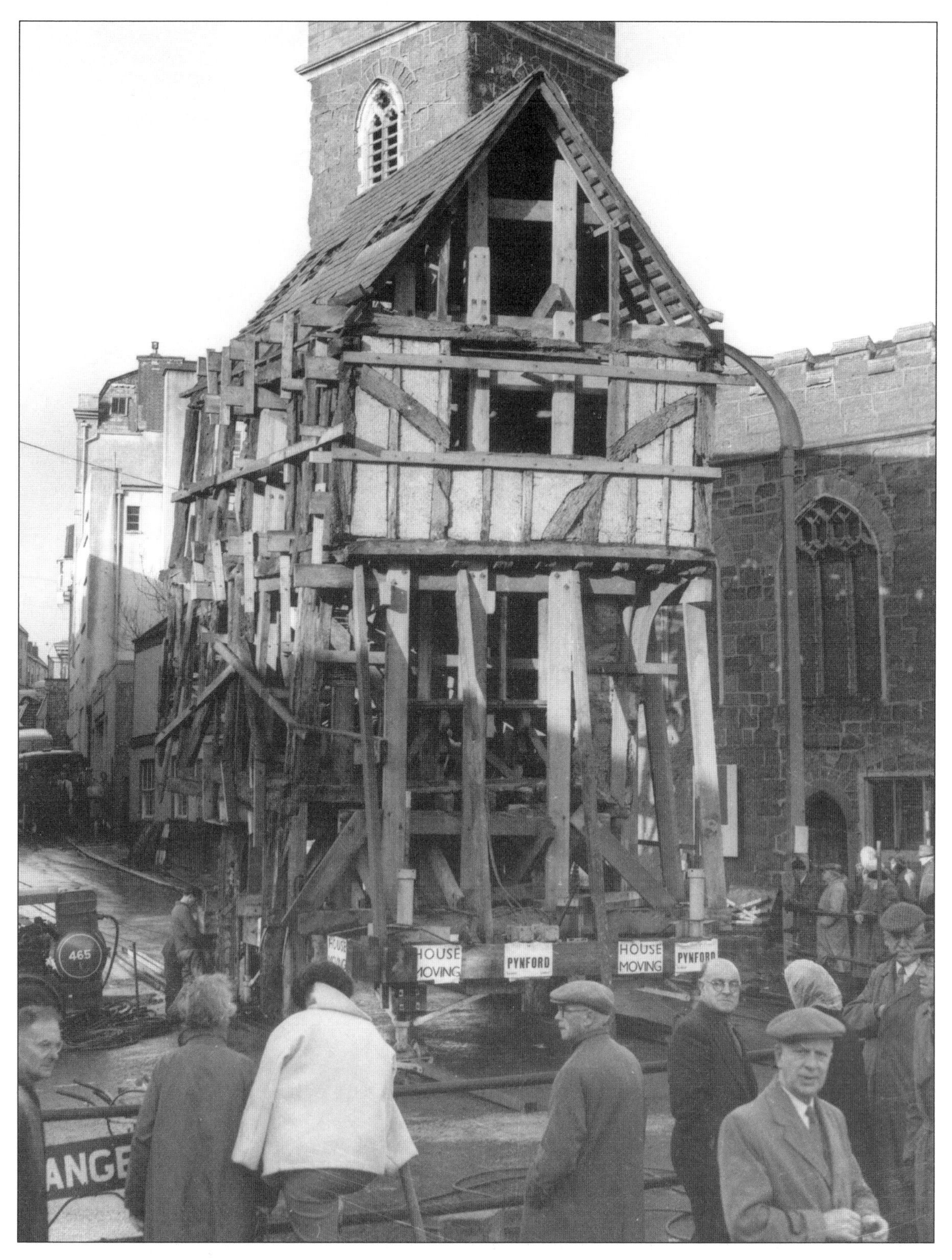

By 12 December 1961 the house was poised to be inserted into its new position adjacent to the City Wall and the site of the old West Gate.

Two days later No. 16 Edmund Street was finally positioned on its new site and the work of restoration could begin. The property had now been given a new name, 'The House That Moved'. Ironically, the site that had been chosen by the City Planning Officer had in fact once been occupied by a building of the same age and style but demolished in the early 1940s.

Restoration work took place over several months, utilising material of comparable age and using traditional techniques. The building was, however, never to be used as a dwelling again. Internally very small by modern standards, it was designated for retail use only. The project was criticised by some as 'a gigantic waste of money' but received an award by the Civic Trust who designated it as 'making an outstanding contribution to the appearance of the local scene'.

'The House That Moved', photographed at night in 1981, commemorating the twentieth year of its move.

Alphington Street and Cowick Street

With the construction of a new road layout leading up to the new Exeter Bridge North, part of Alphington Street was to be radically altered with the demolition of several buildings. These included the Lloyds Bank branch, built in the early twentieth century, and the National Provincial Bank situated at the beginning of the street, just off Exe Bridge. Behind these buildings was Shooting Marsh Style that ran down the edge of the river.

Below: *Alphington Street is shown from the junction with Haven Road just before its removal. The Royal Oak Inn was on the corner. The well-known garage of Pike & Co. operated from large covered premises opposite and today is the site of the Riverside Leisure Centre.*

Until the early 1960s, Cowick Street, still retained its traditional character, with buildings surviving from the eighteenth and nineteenth centuries. The shop with baskets outside containing fruit was that of florist Mrs V Hodges. Next door at No. 6, 'The St Thomas Ironmongery Stores, Established 1820', also displays its wares in age-old style whilst inviting passers-by to 'Come in and look around'. A narrow covered passageway leads to the rear of the premises and Brownes Court. No. 7 was Baker Tobacconists Ltd. With the demolition of this delightful group of buildings an ancient bay window was saved for posterity. But the loss of this historic part of Cowick Street was tragic as it was one of the last Exeter streets to retain such character.

With the removal of buildings in Cowick Street in the early 1960s the mid-nineteenth century station building was exposed. In 1965 The Victorian Society recommended restoration of the Italianate building but this did not take place until the 1980s, as part of the redevelopment plan for the area and undertaken by Sainsbury's. Although in a good state of repair today the railway building stands empty. The semi-derelict site adjacent to the station became the site for a temporary library, superceded by an £8.5 million leisure centre scheme that also included a department store.

South Gate Area

One of Exeter's most interesting areas had developed at the junction of South Street, Magdalen Street and Holloway Street, around the city's South Gate. The construction of the Inner Bypass and new river bridges was to take approximately eighteen years to complete. It was to decimate the South Gate area and could be classed as one of the worst consequences of the postwar development. Within this area was found early timber-framed buildings, ancient inns, courtyards, Regency buildings, and the City Wall. Most were removed. The start of demolition in the Magdalen Street around 1960 can be seen. The Valiant Soldier pub had been demolished on the corner of Holloway Street, and lower Magdalen Street had been removed.

The large seventeenth-century Valiant Soldier pub at the top of Holloway Street was a popular venue for residents on the south side of the city and had a large rear yard that in earlier times provided good accommodation for horse and carts.

On the west side of Holloway Street, at its junction with Magdalen Street, stood a delightful row of buildings. Beside the Wine and Spirit Vaults, shown advertising Heavitree Ales, was the narrow entrance to Quay Lane. Following the City Wall as it stretched down Quay Hill to the river, its width allowed only one person at a time to pass comfortably.

No. 88 Holloway Street was an early-seventeenth-century building used by Robert C Back, builder, contractor and decorator. He was also an oil and colour merchant. The building is shown in 1962 shortly before demolition.

As the Inner Bypass encroached, the upper end of Magdalen Street, near the Eye Infirmary, was removed. The row of buildings included the original Acorn Inn, a diminutive public house with an original early tiled front, just visible, left. Adjacent to it was a row of early-seventeenth-century properties complete with courtyards. Bowdens Place was contained by internal iron gates. On demolition these were removed and erected at the rear of St Nicholas Priory.

On the north side of Magdalen Street, extending from the junction with South Street to Southernhay, stood a fine row of Regency buildings adjoining a single large house dating from the early 1700s. Sadly, the whole of this site gradually fell into a state of disrepair and, with redevelopment carrying on apace, the buildings were pulled down in 1977.

Bowdens Place, Magdalen Street, prior to its destruction in 1960.

This large property in Magdalen Street was originally built for Dr Dicker around 1727 and named Magdalen House. It was later owned by a wool merchant in the early 1800s. The property was divided in 1868 and shop fronts added. Unique in Exeter, it could have been saved but was instead demolished with its neighbours.

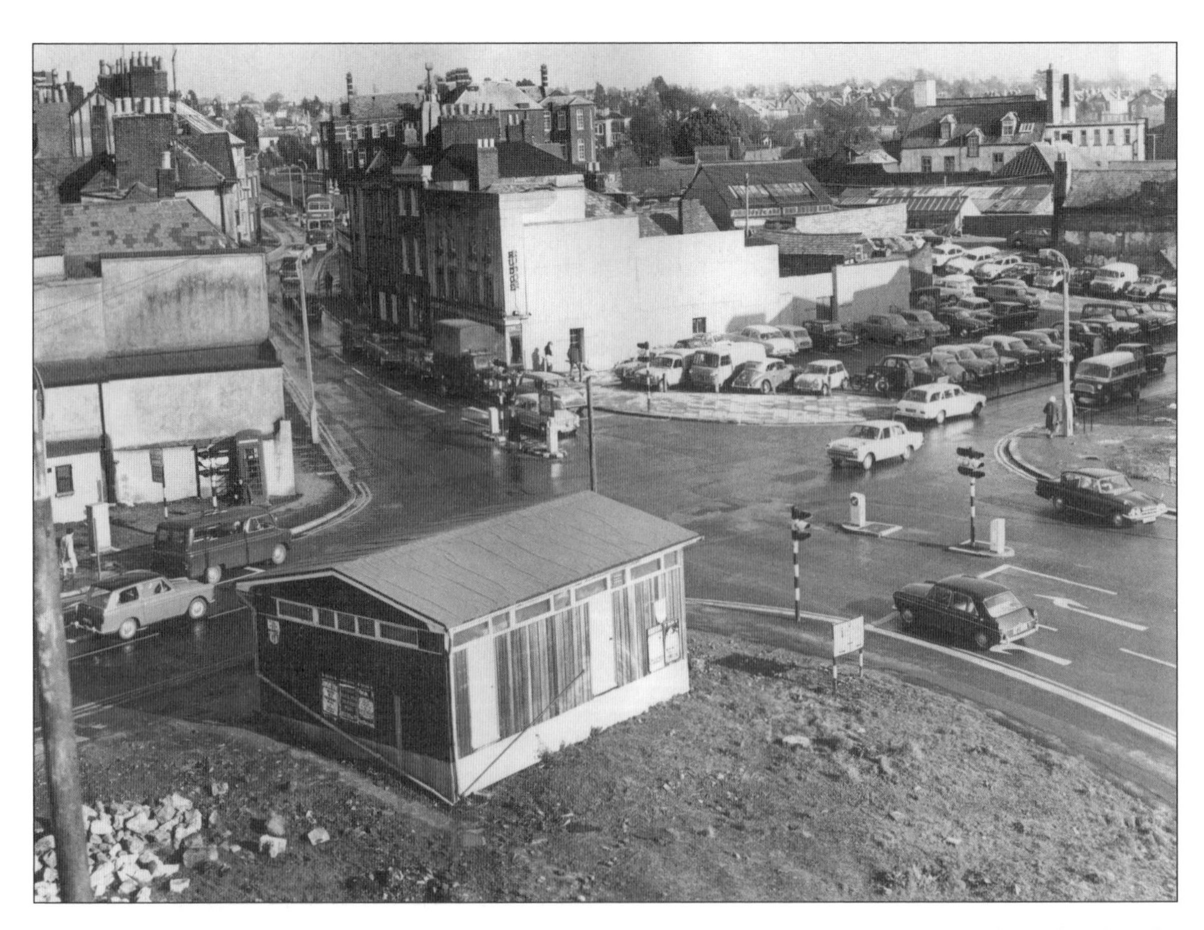

With the building of Western Way the area at South Gate was opened up and a temporary shop placed at the junction. The site of the Valiant Soldier became a car park. Shown in 1967 it was to be a short time before this section of Magdalen Street was knocked down.

The Magdalen Street site was named 'The Acorn' after the one-time pub there. In 1967 the road system was changed and a new Acorn Inn built off the road and nearer the Eye Infirmary. It was decided to construct another road skirting the pub, to help the traffic flow. In The Friars older buildings were also removed and new flats built. Photo 1968.

The top of Western Way in 1967. To enable the Inner Bypass to continue down to the river a section of the City Wall was removed. Permission had to be granted by the Ministry of Works and the work recorded. New flats built at the bottom of South Street had a fine view over the City Wall as it continued down to the Quay.

In Holloway Street a variety of buildings ran along the south side to join with Magdalen Street. A row of large Victorian properties with front gardens stretched from Melbourne Street to The Friars. Having succumbed to neglect, they were eventually cleared to allow the street to be widened. Photo c.*1965.*

End of an era – a digger finishes off the demolition of Victorian houses in Holloway Street.

The narrow entry to Quay Hill leading from Holloway Street.

Below: *The corner of Magdalen Street with South Street, showing Nos 36 to 39 c.1960. The buildings that backed on to Trinity Street were to be demolished and became the site for the Forte Hotel (today the South Gate Hotel).*

In September 1969 the medieval courtyard complex of buildings in Magdalen Street called Wynards Almshouses was closed but with ideas to turn it into an arts centre. The last resident was one of Exeter's well-known characters, eighty-year-old Clarence Elvin. He was often seen selling flags for charity but for many of Exeter's children Clarence 'was' Father Christmas. For many years he took on the role at the popular High Street store Waltons. The company created Fairyland each year and Clarence had the best set of real whiskers of any Santa. He is recorded by the author just before leaving his home at Wynards in 1969.

Trinity Street

Trinity Street took its name from Holy Trinity Church, today known as, the White Ensign Club. The church stands near the site of the old South Gate, abutting the City Wall. On the south side was Trinity Street, a narrow thoroughfare that joined Southernhay West. At its entrance was a cluster of buildings including a small warehouse. Further up, cottages with small back gardens lined the City Wall. Pre-war the street was pedestrian-only, being too narrow for vehicles. Postwar the South Gate area was opened up and a wall built in front of the church integrating the bronze wall plaque relating to the City Gate.

Nos 14 and 15 Trinity Street were later demolished. The cottages stood facing the disused Trinity Green Burial Yard opposite the Royal Devon and Exeter Hospital. It had been a burial ground for cholera victims in the early-nineteenth century.

The car park at Trinity Street was partly built over the seventeenth-century graveyard that had been closed after the cholera epidemic of 1832. The line of evergreen oaks marked its original boundary. A new shelter and public convenience were built in conjunction with the car park and, seen top right, is the very narrow entrance to Trinity Street and adjacent to it coach builders A G Dowell & Sons .

James Street – Loss of an Old Back Street

James Street connected South Street and Coombe Street. The entrance, which still exists, is found opposite George's Meeting in South Street but the access from Coombe Street no longer exists having been removed to create a car park for the White Hart Hotel. The L-shaped street, lined with houses, was flanked by the City Wall on its south side and it is seen at the top of the street in this photograph, as seen from Coombe Street. Part of the street suffered war damage in May 1942 but most of the properties escaped destruction. The loss of buildings that abutted the City Wall allowed local children to scale the structure and look down on the back gardens of cottages on Quay Hill.

For children living in the area of Magdalen Street, Holloway Street and The Friars, James Street provided a good short cut to Central School. The local Victorian school overlooked Coombe Street and can just be seen at the end of the street.

The whole of James Street was destroyed in the construction of the Inner Bypass. In removing the street in the early 1960s some interesting eighteenth-century properties, were pulled down. This fine building, well worthy of restoration, stood at the bottom of James Street before turning towards Coombe Street.

Mary Arches Street

Mary Arches Street takes its name from the church and its Norman arches. Pre-war it was the civic church for Exeter. The street was originally narrow, leading from Fore Street opposite the Lower Market to Bartholomew Street. After the war it still retained an intimate character, with three period dwellings adjacent to the church, as shown by this aerial view taken in the mid-1950s. In the foreground is the Mint Methodist Church and beside it two warehouses formerly owned by Brocks Furnishers; to the right is St Olave's Church, Fore Street. The street widened at the church, known locally as St Mary Arches Square. Off the Square to the right, adjacent to the three houses was Synagogue Place, that still retains one of the oldest synagogues in the country. The Gaumont Cinema is shown behind and, to the left, Mary Arches Street Infants' School (later demolished).

St Mary Arches Street with properties that were demolished in the early 1960s. The building shown centre was occupied by Len Born, cycle agent and repairs. Next door is the London Electrical Wire Co. & Smiths.

Nos 50, 51 and 52 Mary Arches Street, all demolished in 1960s.

The premises of Len Born, now Motor & Motor Cycle Repairs, shown before demolition c.*1960.*

Golden Heart Project

The origin of the name Waterbeer Street relates to the waterbearers who sold water for one penny a bucket. The narrow backstreet running parallel with High Street extended from Goldsmith Street to North Street. Until 1960 it was very much intact but within a short period of time it was to be decimated.

In 1960 the Victorian Gothic police station, built in 1880, was removed as part of the concept for creating a new shopping area in Exeter. Unique in style, the building was conveniently situated behind the Guildhall where courts were held. To one side of the building was Pancras Lane, a short cut to Paul Street.

In the foyer of the police station was a section of an original Roman mosaic that had been relaid into the floor and had undergone some restoration work. On demolition of the building the mosaic was lifted and retained by the Royal Albert Museum but at some later date was inadvertently destroyed.

Almost opposite the police station, at Nos 14–16 Waterbeer Street, was ironmongers Edwin Munk. By 1960 the building was showing definite signs of wear and tear, as seen by this record. It was taken over by another ironmongers, Walter Otton, in the early 1960s and later in the 80s by an optician.

The interior of E I Munk in Waterbeer Street.

A large brick five-storeyed building was used as the Court House Annexe, next to the police station, of which this may be one of the only records. All buildings on the north side of Waterbeer Street were demolished for rebuilding in the early 1960s.

The Castle Café run by S T & G T Mountain was a popular venue in Waterbeer Street in the 1950s and 60s.

Goldsmith Street, running from High Street to Paul Street, was to be radically changed by plans for Exeter's new shopping centre. The new Golden Heart Project destroyed the old street, leaving just one building standing. The entry from High Street shows Waltons' store and the original arched façade of the Phoenix Inn, left. It was pulled down and recreated as a replica over the side service entrance for Marks & Spencer.

The convenient narrow thoroughfare of Goldsmith Street gave a short cut to the bus station in Paul Street. Numerous period buildings lined this street including jewellers, butchers, grocers, pubs, hairdressers and estate agents.

Conveniently, Goldsmith Street backed on to the rear of the 1838 Higher Market whose structure dominated the north end of the street. To the right is shown the Wool Hall of the woollen cloth merchants Leare, Brown & Dunsford. It was later to be removed and its façade replicated, becoming the entrance into Marks & Spencer from Goldsmith Street.

The Higher Market rear entrance is shown with its original railings and steps in Goldsmith Street. Redevelopment destroyed the classical proportion of the façade by significantly raising the ground level.

St John Ambulance Association operated from St John's House in Goldsmith Street until the mid-1960s.

Waterbeer Street, as seen in 1960, looking to High Street, from the rear entrance of the Higher Market.

The Higher Market closed in September 1962 and was left awaiting its fate for a number of years. The structure was eventually internally transformed and integrated into the new Guildhall Shopping Centre. Photo 1962.

Interior of the Higher Market, after closure in 1962.

The arcade of the Higher Market was to lose its airy atmosphere after being divided into shop units as part of the redevelopment.

The Civic Hall, next to the Higher Market in Queen Street, was closed and the interior pulled down in 1970. Opened around 1920, it had survived for fifty years. It was later replaced by St George's Hall in Fore Street.

A packed house in the Civic Hall in the 1950s.

Aerial view of the Golden Heart Project site, before start of building.

Waterbeer Street and the area incorporating St Pancras Lane was used as a car park after removal of existing buildings, entry being from Paul Street. To the right is seen the side wall of the extensive Garton & King Foundry, also later removed. Photo 1966.

Entry from Paul Street into the car park at Waterbeer Street.

The site of Waterbeer Street is seen after removal of buildings on the north side, showing the rear of the Guildhall, left, The Turks Head and Brooking & Son. The rear of St Pancras Church is seen right.

The removal of buildings in Goldsmith Street exposes the rear aspect of the Higher Market.

The ancient church of St Pancras narrowly escaped demolition and was eventually fenced off during building works on the Golden Heart Project.

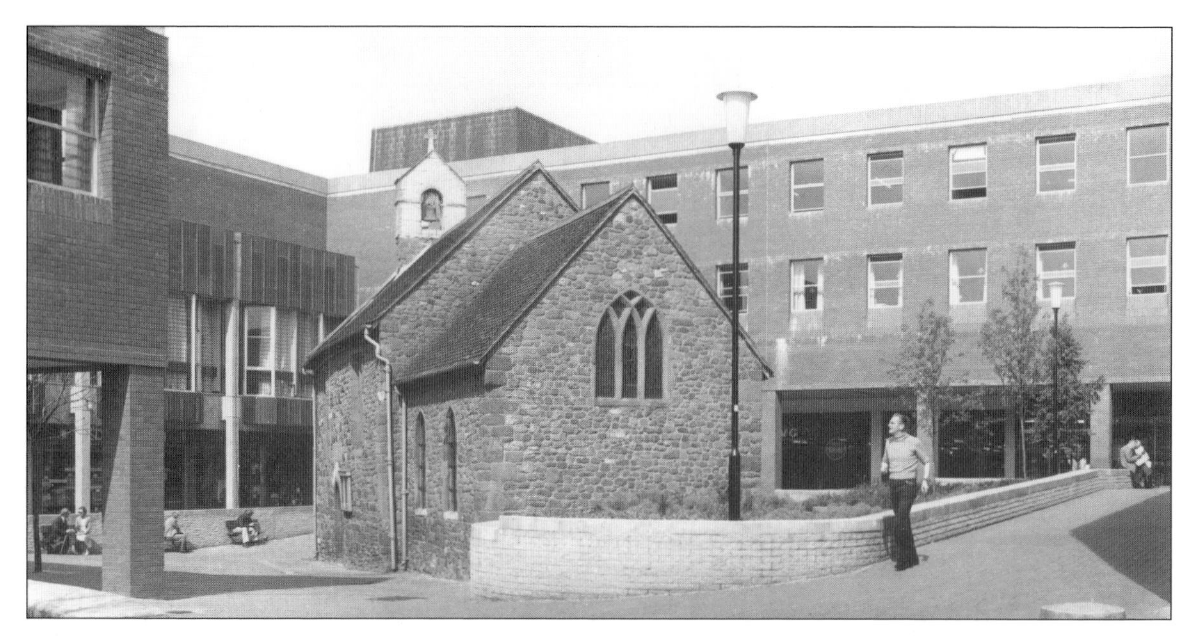

St Pancras Church was left surrounded by unsympathetic and bland architecture.

Waterbeer Street rebuilt, looking from south to east.

Rebuilt Waterbeer Street from east to west.

A small garden, incorporating the foundation stone of the old police station as a cornerstone, was laid out at the heart of Waterbeer Street and the new shopping centre A sculpture titled 'Looking Forward' was created for the site by Exeter sculptor Peter Thursby to commemorate the silver jubilee of Her Majesty the Queen, and unveiled on 30 September 1977.

The massive scale of the new Golden Heart Project demonstrably failed to take account of the city's variety of architecture and townscape.

An insensitive approach to blending new styles of architecture mars the view of Exeter's most important attraction.

An aerial view c.1960 shows the extent of the central area that was to be redeveloped for the Golden Heart Project. The road shown central left is Paul Street and to the right, North Street. It is bounded by Queen Street, top, and High Street, right, running diagonally. The large covered building off Queen Street is the Higher Market and centrally placed Waterbeer Street Car Park. Nearly every building shown was demolished. To the left is shown Paul Street Bus and Coach Station, later to be replaced with the Harlequin Shopping Centre.

Theatre Royal and Barnfield Theatre

The history of Exeter's Theatre Royal was a colourful one, not only because of the preformances and number ofartistes it hosted but because of its fateful connection with fire. The first Theatre Royal, in Bedford Street, was destroyed by fire in 1820, as was its successor in 1885. Exeter's theatre moved to a new site at the junction of Longbrook Street and New North Road. Two years' later, in 1887, fire once again ravaged the theatre in a tragedy that claimed the lives of 187 people – and again it was rebuilt. It is seen here in 1958, showing the pantomime Cinderella.

The interior of the Theatre Royal, Exeter, was designed to hold 1500 people, and following refurbishments at the turn of the century was decorated with six large wall murals, seen right. Work was undertaken on theatre sets by F J Widgery, one of Exeter's best-known artists.

As the Theatre Royal went into decline, a decision was made to sell off the building. In 1962 the last show took place, devised by well-known pantomime 'dame' 'Clarkson Rose' who had appeared many times at the theatre. It was a summer production, entitled Twinkle, *and the curtain finally fell on 22 September.*

The Theatre Royal attracted a variety of famous entertainers and actors and was for a long period of time a vital aspect of the cultural life of the city. Clarkson Rose was one of England's most famous panto dames and supported the theatre to the very last day.

For the audience, the fire curtain was an item of interest in its own right as an advertising board for local companies. This curtain features, from top left, Naden Cycles, May's Fish Restaurant, Edith Haughton, ladies' wear, Tecalemit, motor maintenance, Dollar Beer, Sherriffs Buttery, Express Cleaners, Dart & Bernard, photography, Mitchells, jewellers, Gaytons Garage, Arch Matthews, turf accountants, Luxitax Car Hire and Greenslade's Tours.

Telephone 4021

THEATRE ROYAL
EXETER

Proprietors: EXETER THEATRE CO., LTD.

Licensee and General Manager: T. C. GWILLIAM

SEASON
OF
OPERA PLAYS
VARIETY REVUE
MUSICAL ATTRACTIONS

★

ADMISSION PRICES—*including Tax*
Orchestra Stalls, 6/-; Stalls, 4/6 and 3/6; Pit Stalls, 2/6; Pit, 1/6; Dress Circle, 6/-; Circle, 4/6 and 3/6; Boxes for 4 persons, 24/-, ; for 3 persons 18/-

Times of Performances:
Monday to Thursday Evenings at 7.30 p.m.
Friday and Saturday at 5 p.m. and 8 p.m.

TWICE NIGHTLY Performances for VARIETY and REVUE—6 p.m. and 8.30 p.m.

Admission Prices for Twice Nightly Performances:—5/-, 4/6, 4/-, 3/6, 2/6 and 1/6

The Theatre Royal, built in 1889, was demolished in July 1963 and the site acquired for development.

The Theatre Royal site was acquired by Prudential Assurance as a new office block, shown in 1979.

Originally part of Barnfield House, the Barnfield Theatre's premises were once used by the Exeter Literary Society who occupied the site from 1883. A large lecture hall and annexe were created. The building was used for meetings and lectures until the Society hit financial problems, and it was sold off in the late 1930s. Several uses later, the Exeter Little Theatre Company approached the City Council to convert it back to a theatre and it reopened after a refurbishment in October 1976.

Dix's Field

Dix's Field, constructed in the early-nineteenth century, was one of Exeter's most prestigious developments, built by architect Matthew Nosworthy on an excellent central location. Southernhay Congregational Church was added in 1868. The fine terraces were severely damaged during the blitz of May 1942 and are shown gutted on the south side, with three properties remaining in the south-east corner. Three buildings also survived on the east side. The main body of the church was gutted but its tower and spire survived.

Below: *Dix's Field is shown looking from the south. All gutted buildings were demolished, with only the original south-east corner remaining. These were later restored and the terrace recreated, maintaining the attractive appearance. The old line of Paris Street still remained at this period but was later changed towards the west.*

This aerial view from the early 1960s shows the south side of Dix's Field in use as a car park following demolition of the mostly gutted terrace. Southernhay Congregational Church had been completely rebuilt, retaining the original tower. Three properties still remained on the north side of Dix's Field. The new Paris Street roundabout had been completed and the bus station was in operation.

In 1964 the entry into Dix's Field still retained its fine original lamp standards but the area was utilised for a car park on the south side. A small pay kiosk operated from the middle of the road.

Sidwell Street

Pre-war, Standfield & White motor mechanics operated a garage from No. 8 Sidwell Street and were agents for Rootes Group, Humber, Hillman, Sunbeam, Talbot, Commer and Karrier. The corner of the London Inn Square and Sidwell Street was destroyed by fire during the blitz of May 1942. However, the company continued their operations from the same site until it was acquired for the building of the largest department store in Exeter, Bobby & Co.

Sidwell Street was to be radically changed with postwar development. Whilst the upper half of the street was devastated in 1942 the lower part from St Sidwell's Church to the London Inn Square survived intact. This part of the street featured a variety of architectural styles, together with some buildings of historic interest. Redevelopment removed all the existing standing buildings leaving the seven-storey department store to dominate the skyline. The start of demolition is shown on the north side, c.*1960.*

A pleasing group of buildings was demolished in 1960. The construction of Bobby's is continuing behind the properties.

Removing buildings on the south side of Sidwell Street c.*1960.*

A well-known period building dating from 1820 was demolished on the lower north side of lower Sidwell Street, to make way for a new monolithic block. At this time the shops were occupied by Edna Sherrell, florists, Force & Sons, estate agents, and Shaul Konditori, bakers, and later Lipton's and the Pram & Toy Shop. Photo c.*1960.*

W French & Co., Est 1833, specialised in seeds, fertilisers, garden sundries and poultry foods, and operated from a shop on the south side of Sidwell Street next to the Victory Inn. The company set up temporary premises in the early-postwar years on an empty adjacent site.

Poltimore Square, an enclosed area of dwellings, was typical of buildings found in the Sidwell Street area. These properties were removed for the building of Bobby's department store (now Debenhams).

The proposed plan for the top of Paris Street leading into Sidwell Street.

The new Bobby & Co. department store dominates the city skyline in central Exeter, as seen from High Street. Photo mid-1960s.

Sidwell Street after rebuilding in 1979.

North Street and Exe Street

In the postwar period North Street still retained at No. 38 a unique building that was certainly one of the most important of its period in the city. On the east side of the street, adjacent to the Elephant Inn, it was recognisable by its decorative seventeenth-century frontage. A fine plaster ceiling of the same period could be seen on the first floor. However, the building, originally a merchant's house, dated from the fifteenth century. North Street was earmarked for demolition on the east side to make way for the new Guildhall Shopping Centre. Once vacated by it owners, Mansfield's Antique Dealers, No. 38 was the subject of an archaeological investigation. This established that the building was not fake, as had been suggested by some, but had been carefully altered over a period of time whilst retaining its earliest features. Despite this, No. 38, was, unfortunately, demolished in 1972.

Above: *The seventeenth-century plaster ceiling on the first floor of No. 38.*

Right: *The medieval wooden gallery in the inner court was unique in Exeter. Large stone fireplaces, wall paintings and other historic features were found.*

Below the Iron Bridge and off Exe Street stood a delightful group of buildings known as 'Toby's Court'. The exterior ground was cobbled with an open gutter and originally had been just off the road leading to the North Gate before the building of the Iron Bridge in 1834. This area was a popular stopping-off place for people coming to market and at one time featured several hostelries, such as the Angel Inn, the Spotted Dog, Crown and Sceptre, the Falcon Inn, Black Dog Inn and the Plume of Feathers. All the buildings shown were removed in the early 1960s.

Toby's Court and local residents c.1920.

The Building of C&A

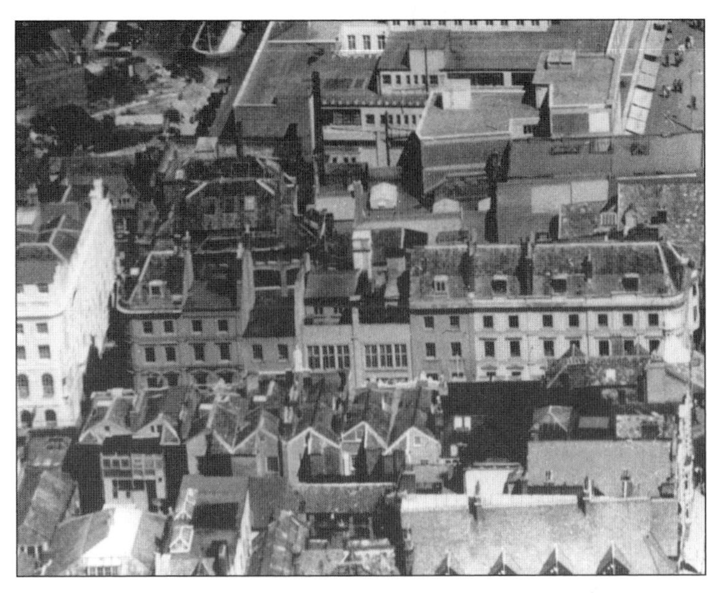

The junction of Queen Street with High Street had been recognised as a most important and architecturally sensitive part of the High Street in postwar Exeter. The eastern side of Queen Street had consisted of an extensive run of mid-nineteenth-century buildings extending to Little Queen Street, until a section was removed and rebuilt in the early-twentieth century. The original designs had been subject to rigorous scrutiny to ensure that the site was appropriately developed by its owner Revd Nathaniel Cole. With the proposals to upgrade the site in the 1970s the opportunity existed to reinstate the dignity of these properties, maintaining and enhancing the look of the street. Instead, a decision was taken to demolish the whole block. This would lead to the construction of one of the most inappropriately designed buildings in the city.

The nineteenth-century frontage of Nathaniel Cole's building curved gracefully around the corners of Little Queen Street and High Street. An opportunity existed to further enhance and restore these important buildings but was lost. Interestingly, on the opposite side the new Marks & Spencer building was to reflect the earlier architectural styles of buildings that had been lost but did not succeed in having an overall coordinated design.

The newly constructed building for C & A was to be a highly controversial structure and failed to add any architectural merit to this important junction. Its monotonous design jarred against its historic seventeenth-century neighbours. The site of Waltons had been demolished in this photograph and the construction of Marks & Spencer was about to begin.

New Housing

Toronto House, at Stoke Hill, was built to house people who had lost their homes during the Exeter Blitz in May 1942. The complex of dwellings was opened by HRH Princess Elizabeth on 2 October 1949.

New housing at Dunsford Road in 1960.

A view over the city from the Redhills area, 1962.

READER'S LETTER

Housing Sites— 'Big Items'

Sir,—As a woman I am very interested in the proposed building sites for the much needed houses in Exeter and I am wondering whether the people who will be expected to rent such houses have been considered when the sites have been selected. I have in mind the sites at Countess Wear and Hollow Lane. Have the Council and Housing Committee considered the following points which would be big items for the would-be tenants?

1.—Providing extended 'bus-routes are provided the daily bread-winner would have to travel at least another ten minutes to and from the city further than the present housing sites, which would leave very little time for the mid-day meal during the lunch hour, and what working man can afford lunches in town?

2.—Do the would-be tenants wish to come so far away from the city and their friends, etc.? It is very nice if one owns a car, but when 'bus routes have to be considered, and weather, I personally think there are many housewives who would prefer to live nearer Exeter. Country life is all right for those who like it.

3.—The point was raised at the meeting of the City Council that one of the proposed sites was "unhealthy and rheumaticy." This should be investigated further before the land is acquired.

Surely there are building sites nearer the city which could be used for the proposed sites, and I think several smaller sites would be preferable to two or three large ones so far removed from the city proper and where 'bus fares and travelling time would not be extra considerations for the tenants.

"INTERESTED WELL-WISHER."
Exeter.

Housing redevelopment at Newtown, 1969.

Media interviews relating to housing at Newtown, c.1969.

Barley Mount, Exwick, 1962.

Start of building in Exwick, c.*1978.*

The Shilhay Housing project provoked controversy in the 1970s.

New flats are built in Sidwell Street, 1966.